How Sweet Are Thy Words

Also by Gleniece Lytle

Hearts Unto Wisdom

How Sweet Are Thy Words

**The Curious Woman's Guide to
Delightful Discovery of What the KJV
Bible's Unusual Words
*Actually Mean***

Gleniece Lytle

Desert Rain Editions

How Sweet Are Thy Words: The Curious Woman's Guide to Delightful Discovery of What the KJV Bible's Unusual Words Actually Mean

Copyright © 2025 by Gleniece Lytle

ISBN: 979-8-9910681-3-0 (paprback) 979-8-9910681-2-3 (ebook)

Published by Desert Rain Editions, LLC

https://desertraingleniece.com

https://desertrainediting.com

Unless otherwise marked, all Scripture is taken from the *Holy Bible King James Version* (KJV).

All Bible word definitions are taken from *Strong's Exhaustive Concordance of the Bible: Updated Addition*, Massachusetts, Hendrickson Publishers, 2007.

Further research where noted used *Vine's Complete Expository Dictionary of Old and New Testament Words*, © 1984, 1996, Thomas Nelson, Inc., Nashville, TN.

Note: Bible verses marked by bold italics or words within square brackets were added for emphasis and explanation throughout this study.

Thank you Janet Nash for your earlier imput, to Connie Harten for your extensive reading and feedback, and to Lika Angel for your helpful beta-read throughout. All of you are gems.

Open book with flowers image courtesy of Natworanat via Canva.

To my fellow curious Christian women

And to my dearest husband. You are loved beyond my humble words. I will see you in the kingdom.

Contents

Introduction

I love the King James Version Bible. I believe it is one of the most accurate and beautiful translation we can read. Nevertheless, it is important for us to know that none of the translations we have today, including the King James Version (KJV), is perfect. Only the original Hebrew and Greek texts from which they came were divinely inspired.

The KJV, its lyrical beauty aside, employs several antiquated words, and words that have changed their meanings over time, that might send us scrambling for the nearest dictionary or concordance. In this book, I take words that we may be unfamiliar with outside their biblical setting or that may be confusing to our modern-day English sensibilities, and expound upon their original meanings within the context of the verse.

I have always been a curious woman. Curiosity has pushed me to ask: *What is it? How does it work? What does it mean? Why is it the way it is?* and *How did it come to be?* In grade school, I read every library resource I could find on the Loch Ness Monster, Bigfoot, the Abominable Snowman, and the Bermuda Triangle but was totally bummed to find out there wasn't a concrete answer. Sometimes, the answers are hidden, forever to remain a mystery until Christ returns. Certain cultural, historical, or end-times passages found in the Bible are no different.

But when it comes to unusual words and their meanings, we have a dedicated scholar to thank for his amazing life achievement in creating a profound and extensive concordance of the Bible—James Strong. This tome, *Strong's Exhaustive Concordance of the Bible*, is indispensable for understanding the etymology of the various words I researched for this book, and is what I reached for when confused or just plain curious about a word's usage in my study of the KJV Bible. Another helpful resource I used was *Vine's Complete Expository Dictionary of Old and New Testament Words*.

It is my hope each chapter of this book brings you clarity and broadens your understanding of many beloved yet obscure KJV Bible passages. For your convenience, I have included in each chapter a section of the dictionary entry from *Strong's Concordance*. In these charts, the Hebrew and Greek definitions are numbered and listed in the order they appear in the Bible from Genesis through Revelation and not in numerical order. In each numbered entry, you will find the Hebrew- or Greek-to-English spelling of the word followed by its meaning, and then by this symbol :— which indicates the various ways the KJV translates the word. Note: I retained the original *Strong's Concordance* British English spelling for all entry definitions.

Throughout the Bible, especially the New Testament, one word may be used in several contexts (see chapter 15, Sober), so it's imperative to know which definition for that identical word was meant for that specific verse. Therefore, I often added in brackets the *Strong's* number within the particular Bible verse I chose to share.

Being a curious Christian woman, I love a good word study. It is my hope that you, with your God-given curiosity, glean some additional insight into the rich words used in the KJV Bible.

How sweet are thy words unto my taste! yea, sweeter than honey to my mouth! (Psalm 119:103)

[1]

Admonish

*Let the word of Christ dwell in you richly in all wisdom; teaching and **admonishing** one another in psalms and hymns and spiritual songs, singing with grace in your hearts to the Lord. (Colossians 3:16)*

We Christians have a sacred duty to admonish our fellow brethren out of love and a desire for their good. But in order to do this well, we need to understand exactly what is being asked of us. Looking up this word in *Strong's Concordance* shows us that *admonish* (or one of its derivatives *admonished*, *admonishing*, and *admonition*) is found twelve times in the King James Version Bible. Paul spoke these words of praise to the brethren in Romans:

And I myself also am persuaded of you, my brethren, that ye also are full of goodness, filled with all knowledge, able also to admonish one another. (Romans 15:14)

Admonish

G3560 *noutheteō*; to *put in mind*, to *caution*, or *reprove gently*:— warn

Admonished H2094 *zāthar*; to *gleam*, figuratively to *enlighten* (by caution):— teach, shine, give warning

H5749 *ûd*; to *duplicate* or *repeat*; by implication to *protest*, *testify*:— bear witness, charge, give warning

G3867 *paraineō*; to *mispraise*, i.e. *recommend* or *advise* (a different course):— exhort

G5537 *chrēmatizō*; to *utter an oracle*, i.e. divinely *intimate*; *bear* as a *title*:— be called, (warned) of God, reveal, speak

Admonishing G3560: see definition above

Admonition G3559 *nouthesia*; calling *attention* to, i.e. (by implication) mild *rebuke* or *warning*

The meaning of admonish (G3560) in Romans 15:14, 1 Thessalonians 5:12, and 2 Thessalonians 3:15 is to "put in mind, caution, reprove gently, or warn." But before we can caution or reprove anyone, we need to be able to judge (or discern) between right and wrong. We need to be in God's Word. We need to be, as Paul said in Romans, filled with the goodness and knowledge of Christ in order to admonish rightly.

Nobody lives their life perfectly. And nobody likes to be told that they are at fault or straying from the truth. But as Christians, it is our duty to point out with love biblical errors or actions we see that might cause spiritual harm to our fellow brethren. If we witness behavior or hear words that go against biblical teaching and turn our heads away (i.e., tolerate), we are not showing love. We are perpetuating sin, and allowing our fear of man to be more powerful than our fear of God.

Better is a poor and wise child, than an old and foolish king, who will no more be admonished.
(Ecclesiastes 4:13)

The definition of admonished (H2094) in Ecclesiastes 4:13 and again in Ecclesiastes 12:12 means to "gleam, shine [as a spotlight, perhaps?], enlighten by caution, give warning." Ecclesiastes 4:13 makes it known there were people willing to listen to instruction *at one time*, but they allowed their authority, credentials, wealth, age, or experience to puff them up, and they refused to heed instruction any longer. Because of their status and material advances, they see themselves above godly enlightenment. How tragic. There is never a point in our physical lives where we attain all knowledge or can claim to have "arrived."

> *The Lord hath said concerning you, O ye remnant*
> *of Judah; Go ye not into Egypt: know certainly that*
> *I have admonished you this day. (Jeremiah 42:19)*

God sent the prophet Jeremiah to admonish (H5749) Judah, or to "testify against them, witness, protest, and charge." Yet, did Judah heed the warning? No, they did not.

> *And now I have this day declared it to you; but ye*
> *have not obeyed the voice of the Lord your God, nor*
> *any thing for the which he hath sent me unto you.*
> *(Jeremiah 42:21)*

Sadly, refusal to listen and repent was a pattern with Israel and Judah. Let it not be so with us.

The only instance of the word *admonished* with the G5537 definition meaning to "utter an oracle, [be] warned of God" is found in Hebrews where

> *Moses was admonished of God when he was about to*
> *make the tabernacle: for, See, saith he, that thou make*
> *all things according to the pattern shewed to thee in*
> *the mount. (Hebrews 8:5)*

In Acts 27:9, Paul admonished (G3867) or "recommended or advised a different course" of action to the men in charge of the ship he and two hundred and seventy-six other men were sailing on in the Mediterranean Sea.

> *Now when much time was spent, and when sailing*
> *was now dangerous ... Paul admonished them,*
> *And said unto them, Sirs, I perceive this voyage will*
> *be with hurt and much damage, not only of the lading*
> *and ship, but also of our lives. (Acts 27:9–10)*

We women often admonish the G3867 way in our day-to-day discourse. We recommend or advise a different course of action to our husbands about the family finances, our children's education, best places to shop, when to book appointments, and our shared plans for the future. This is not done with force, but with thoughtful respect to a husband's leadership role.

Lastly, we have the word *admonition* (G3559). The Greek noun *nouthesia* used in Ephesians 6:4, Titus 3:10, and in 1 Corinthians 10:11 means "calling attention to, a mild rebuke or warning." As wives with godly husbands, it's a pretty sure guarantee we've been admonished by them at some point. It doesn't feel good to have our spiritual doubts, missteps, and wanderings exposed, but good husbands will understand their God-given responsibility to us and speak up—and we grow as women of God because of it. Their gentle reminders for us to stand strong and not give in to the discontent and faithless mindset that creeps into our being is what admonition is all about. Caring enough to correct. Likewise, as mothers, it is our God-given responsibility to guide and correct our children. We do this out of care for their physical lives, but more importantly, their spiritual ones. Ephesians 6:4 speaks clearly how we should raise up our children: "And, ye fathers, provoke not your children to wrath; but bring them up in the nurture and admonition of the Lord."

> *Now all these things happened unto them for ensamples: and they are written for our admonition, upon whom the ends of the world are come.*
> *(1 Corinthians 10:11)*

Paul called attention to the many ways the Israelites disobeyed God and chose their own path that resulted in their downfall. He did this to warn the brethren he loved. Paul's responsibility to admonish is no different than ours; the body of Christ needs it now more than ever. The Word of God is not subject to our emotions or the current generation's definition of morality. It is our duty to warn fellow sisters who might be fooled by the slick book marketing of supposed Bible teachers whose covers project an illusion of wisdom or answers to their pain but tout a feel-good, anything-goes, pat-yourself-on-the-back theology wrapped in Christianese instead. Warnings were placed in the Bible for a reason because we're all susceptible to deception.

> *For the time will come when they will not endure sound doctrine, but after their own lusts shall they heap to themselves teachers, having itching ears;*
> *And they shall turn away their ears from the truth, and shall be turned into fables. (2 Timothy 4:3–4)*

Be aware of your own spiritual condition and the temptations that surround you, and out of love and deep concern for your sisters in Christ, admonish them well. Admonishing others is a Christ-like act of love. An uncomfortable love at times, but a love nonetheless we shouldn't shirk or ignore for fear of being labeled judgmental. We must be willing to humbly admonish others and most importantly—humbly receive it.

> *Likewise, ye younger, submit yourselves unto the elder. Yea, all of you be subject one to another, and be clothed with humility: for God resisteth the proud, and giveth grace to the humble. (1 Peter 5:5)*

[2]

Beseech

Now, my God, let, I **beseech** *thee, thine eyes be open, and let thine ears be attent unto the prayer that is made in this place. (2 Chronicles 6:40)*

We all want to be heard, right? Whether by God or mankind, we want swift and undivided attention to the cries of our hearts. But like a child grabbing the hand of his father and tug, tug, tugging to show him something so very important, we long most for God's ardent regard.

You may not realize it, but every day you beseech when you reverentially implore God in prayer or when you beckon your spouse, children, or closest friends to consider your words. Of the thirty-five times the word *beseech* is used in the Old Testament, all but six are used to address God. Our beseeching Him is an urgent request and a call for action on His part. A prayer spoken in the inhalation of, "Oh, dear God . . ." A prayer of longing and desperation of, "Oh, would that God . . . !"

Beseech

H4994 *nā* a primitive particle of incitement and entreaty, usually rendered *I pray, now* or *then*; added mostly to verbs or interjections:— I pray thee, I pray you, go to, now, oh

H577 *onnā* from H4994; *oh now!*:— I beseech thee, O; I pray thee, O

G3870 *parakaleō*; to *call near*, i.e. *invite, invoke* (by *imploration, exhortation,* or *consolation*):— call for, (be of good) comfort, desire, exhort, (give) exhortation, entreat, pray

G1189 *deomai*; to *beg* (as *binding oneself*), i.e. *petition*:— pray (to), make request

G2065 *erōtaō*; to *interrogate*; by implication to *request*:— ask, desire, intreat, pray

Beseeching G3870 and **G2065**: See definitions above

Pardon, I beseech thee, the iniquity of this people according unto the greatness of thy mercy, and as thou hast forgiven this people, from Egypt even unto now. (Numbers 14:19)

Save now, I beseech thee, O Lord: O Lord, I beseech thee, send now prosperity. (Psalm 118:25)

Wherefore they cried unto the Lord, and said, We beseech thee, O Lord, we beseech thee, let us not perish for this man's life, and lay not upon us innocent blood: for thou, O Lord, hast done as it pleased thee. (Jonah 1:14)

Six of the Old Testament uses of *beseech* are respectful addresses to someone in authority: a king, a captain, a higher official, even a prophet. In Jeremiah chapter 42, all the captains of the remnant of Israel and all the people great and small came to the prophet Jeremiah saying,

Let, we beseech thee, our supplication be accepted before thee, and pray for us unto the Lord thy God even for all this remnant . . .
That the Lord thy God may shew us the way wherein we may walk, and the thing that we may do. (Jeremiah 42:2–3)

In the New Testament, there are thirty-one entries of *beseech* or *beseeching* divided into three similar yet distinct variations for the word. According to *Vine's Complete*

Expository Dictionary of Old and New Testament Words, the Greek word *parakaleō* (G3870) means to "call to one's side" or "call to one's aid." Beseeching is stronger than mere asking. It is an invitation, calling someone near with the intent to comfort them or plead with them or share with them a desire.

Paul wrote to his friend Philemon a plea of love concerning the runaway slave, Onesimus, who had become Paul's beloved brother in Christ. "I beseech thee for my son Onesimus whom I have begotten in my bonds" (Philemon 1:10). In another appeal for the sake of love, Paul addressed the congregation at Corinth:

> *Now I beseech you, brethren, by the name of our Lord Jesus Christ, that ye all speak the same thing, and that there be no divisions among you; but that ye be perfectly joined together in the same mind and in the same judgment. (1 Corinthians 1:10)*

From the Greek word *deomai* (G1189), beseech is rendered to "beg or petition for an urgent need." In Luke 9, the heart of this father was consumed by an urgent need he knew only Jesus Christ could appease.

> *And behold, a man of the company cried out, saying, Master, I beseech thee, look upon my son: for he is mine only child. (Luke 9:38)*

Do you feel the desperate longing in this father's plea? As women of God, we've all been in this place. Begging for a different outcome, a change of heart, a turning of circumstances. Praying that God would save us.

In Galatians 4, Paul was disheartened to learn that many of those he had taught about the grace and freedom in Christ turned back to a state of bondage to the physical Law. He was like a distraught father who had just found out his teenage children were chasing after the wrong crowd. He's not just asking, he's begging them to hear him because he knew how high the stakes were if they strayed, how eternally important it was that they heed his words. His outcry to their stumbling was, "Brethren, I beseech you [I beg of you], be as I am [follow the example I set for you from the beginning]" (Galatians 4:12).

Those things, which ye have both learned, and received, and heard, and seen in me, do: and the God of peace shall be with you. (Philippians 4:9)

Paul beseeched the brethren often in the letters he wrote to hear him and do the right thing, as he did the two women we read about in Philippians 4:2. He did not want their bickering to spoil the love and harmony that should rule their behavior, and implored them to be of the same mind, to think as Christ would for the greater good. When we beseech those we love, we implore them to listen to reason—God's reason—for their spiritual well-being and peace of mind.

Lastly, of the varied definitions of beseech, we have the Greek word *erōtaō* (G2065), which means "earnestly request, ask, or desire." *Erōtaō* was spoken between equals.

The more common word "ask" (*aiteō*, G154) was used by those in a lesser position than the one who was being petitioned: man to God, child to parent, subject to king. →*An interesting note* that cannot be adequately represented in the English language is that in the Gospels whenever Christ asked anything of His Father, He used *erōtaō*, never *aiteō*, which showed His being on equal footing with God the Father.

Both apostles Paul and Peter, as if beholding a loved one's face between their hands and looking them steadily in the eyes, beseeched the brethren to hear their wisdom and knowledge.

> *I* [Paul] *therefore, the prisoner of the Lord, beseech you that ye walk worthy of the vocation wherewith ye are called,*
> *With all lowliness and meekness, with longsuffering, forbearing one another in love. (Ephesians 4:1–2)*

> *Dearly beloved, I beseech you as strangers and pilgrims, abstain from fleshly lusts, which war against the soul. (1 Peter 2:11)*

The apostle John probably understood the love of God better than anyone. It was his prayer, his greatest desire, that we understand this love to the uttermost.

> *And now I beseech thee, lady, not as though I wrote a new commandment unto thee, but that which we had from the beginning, that we love one another.*

And this is love, that we walk after his [Christ's]
commandments. (2 John 1:5–6)

Let us beseech other women of God to hold fast to the
life-preserving truth of Christ amid the tsunami of
falsehoods spewing from the world, to hold tight, as if
nothing else matters—because nothing else does. We all
have an inborn need to be heard, to bid our loved ones
come closer and hear us. Yet there is no guarantee they
will. But when we beseech God with a pure heart and
humbleness of mind, *He will*. Every time. He promised.

*And it shall come to pass, that before they call, I will
answer; and while they are yet speaking, I will hear.
(Isaiah 65:24)*

[3]

Bowels

I am poured out like water, and all my bones are out of joint: my heart is like wax; it is melted in the midst of my **bowels**. *(Psalm 22:14)*

Anger, fear, love, compassion. Like the bowels of the earth, these emotions run deep and reach down toward the very core of our being. Most recent translations of the Bible use the word *heart* or *affection* in place of the word *bowels* from the King James Version. But bowels (G4698, always in the plural) is actually taken from the Greek *splanchnon* properly defined as "the physical organs of the intestines."

Of the thirty-seven entries of *bowels* found in the Old and New Testaments (KJV), more than half of the entries literally mean "stomach" or "intestines," or having to do with reproduction, as in the words *loins* or *womb*. God told childless Abram concerning his steward: "This shall not be thine heir; but he that shall come forth out of thine own bowels shall be thine heir" (Genesis 15:4).

Bowels

H4578 *mē eh* from an unused root probably meaning to *be soft*; used only in plural the *intestines, abdomen,* figuratively *sympathy*; by implication a *vest*; by extension the *stomach, uterus* (or of men, the seat of generation), the *heart* (figuratively):— belly, heart, womb

H7356 *raham*; *compassion* (in the plural); by extension the *womb* (as *cherishing* the fetus); by implication a *maiden*:— compassion, damsel, tender love, mercy, pity, womb

H7130 *qereb*; properly the *nearest* part, i.e. the *center,* whether literally or figuratively:— among, before, in, inward part, inward thought, midst, out of, through, within self

G4698 *splanchon* probably strengthened from *splēn* (the "spleen"); *intestine* (plural); figuratively *pity* or *sympathy*:— inward affection, tender mercy

But Amasa took no heed to the sword that was in Joab's hand: so he smote him therewith in the fifth rib, and shed out his bowels to the ground, and struck him not again; and he died. (2 Samuel 20:10)

By thee have I been holden up from the womb: thou art he that took me from my mother's bowels: my praise shall be continually of thee. (Psalm 71:6)

There is only one instance of the word *bowels* in the New Testament that has a literal meaning. It is found in the book of Acts and refers to Judas Iscariot.

Now this man purchased a field with the reward of iniquity; and falling headlong, he burst asunder in the midst, and all his bowels gushed out. (Acts 1:18)

To understand the non-literal uses of the word *bowels*, we must go back to ancient Greek and Hebrew cultures. It was common at that time to attribute different internal organs to various emotional conditions.

- ❇ The **head** was the seat of understanding.
- ❇ The **heart** was the seat of affection, courage ("take heart"), and memory (learning by "heart").
- ❇ The **intestines** (bowels) were the seat of pity, mercy, and compassion.
- ❇ The **liver** was the seat of honor.
- ❇ The **spleen** was the seat of passion and anger (closely linked to the word *bowels*, G4698).

❁ The **kidneys** (also known as *reins*, G3629) were the
  seat of conscious joy and grief.
❁ The **loins** were the seat of strength and power.

In our modern society, most of these physical organs
and their corresponding emotions have been rolled into
two main areas: the head (thought) and the heart
(emotion). But perhaps the ancients had it right.

When you think of where we actually *feel* emotional
pain or tender affection, is it not in our stomachs? Those
"butterflies" we feel—nervousness, fear, excitement, desire.
We feel them dancing in the pit of our stomachs. When
we've been betrayed or emotionally damaged it is "gut-
wrenching." It feels like we've been "punched in the gut."
We wrap our arms around our middles and rock back and
forth for self-comfort. We crouch in a ball on our beds to
stay the pain. When we respond to a situation without
thought, strictly from our immediate feelings, we say it is
our "gut reaction" or "gut feeling." And when we believe
something is the right thing to do based on our experience,
we "go with our gut" or "trust our gut." Turmoil, desire,
and longing are all expressed in this word: *bowels*.

> *And Joseph made haste; for his bowels did yearn*
> *upon his brother: and he sought where to weep; and*
> *he entered into his chamber, and wept there.*
> *(Genesis 43:30)*

> *My bowels, my bowels! I am pained at my very*
> *heart; my heart maketh a noise in me; I cannot*

hold my peace, because thou hast heard, O my soul,
the sound of the trumpet, the alarm of war.
(Jeremiah 4:19)

In ancient times, the trumpet call was used to alert townspeople for assembly, to impart important news, or to sound for celebration. But when used to warn impending invasion, it must have been terrifying to hear. What a sinking feeling to know destruction was coming!

Just as there are vital inward parts we cannot pinch off and still live, our spiritual lives are no different. If we restrict the flow of God's Spirit in our being, our capacity to love well and reach out with compassion to our fellow man stagnates.

But whoso hath this world's good, and seeth his brother have need, and shutteth up his bowels of compassion from him, how dwelleth the love of God in him? (1 John 3:17)

Bowels of compassion is emotion married to action that makes a difference in someone's life. If the thought is separated from the action, it is useless.

If a brother or sister be naked, and destitute of daily food,
And one of you say unto them, Depart in peace, be ye warmed and filled; notwithstanding ye give them not those things which are needful to the body; what doth it profit? (James 2:15–16)

Just as we cannot separate our works from our faith as James chapter 2 makes clear, our most intimate heartfelt feelings mean nothing when separated from the truth and wisdom of God. We all have feelings, but if they are not coupled with godly knowledge, those feelings will clog our inmost being like tar. Thick with emotion, we are fooled into thinking what we do is good because it *feels* right. But this is not the mind of Christ. The truth of God's Word must reign first, then grace, mercy, and compassion follow. Weighed down by the heavy cloak of our emotions, we help no one if we tolerate their sins (and our own) and pretend all is well. We only prolong their self-deception and crown our feelings above the lordship of Christ.

Put on therefore, as the elect of God, holy and beloved, bowels of mercies, kindness, humbleness of mind, meekness, longsuffering;
Forbearing one another, and forgiving one another, if any man have a quarrel against any: even as Christ forgave you, so also do ye. (Colossians 3:12–13)

Bowels of mercies is an attribute of Christ that encompasses forgiveness and brotherly love—attributes hard to impart, especially when our "brother" is a frustrating spouse, a difficult co-worker, an antagonistic neighbor, or an uncaring friend. But if Christ dwells in us, we are a new creation. The Spirit of God reminds us of our own shortcomings and gives us the power to reach out in Christ-like fashion to others.

Tender mercy, affection, sympathy, pity, compassion: these are the bowels, the depths of feeling we feel for one another, especially toward our children. We love, protect, and forgive them daily. We see their needs before they ever do. Our heavenly Father does the same for us, yet perfectly. With pity birthed from the deepest love, He showers us with tender mercy we do not deserve. The "bowels of Jesus Christ" spoken of in Philippians 1:8, is the ultimate expression of tender mercy—Christ's willing sacrifice that saved us from ourselves so we may live eternally joyful with Him.

I delight to do thy will, O my God: yea, thy law is within my heart [bowels]. *(Psalm 40:8)*

[4]

Conversation

*But as he which hath called you is holy, so be ye holy in all manner of **conversation**. (1 Peter 1:15)*

When we think of the word *conversation*, we automatically assume what it means. Speech, talking to one another, verbal exchange of thoughts and ideas. But *conversation*, the twenty times the King James Version Bible uses this word, embodies a whole lot more than mere speech.

> *The wicked have drawn out the sword, and have bent their bow, to cast down the poor and needy, and to slay such as be of upright conversation. (Psalm 37:14)*

> *Whoso offereth praise glorifieth me: and to him that ordereth his conversation aright will I shew the salvation of God. (Psalm 50:23)*

Conversation

H1870 *derek*; a *road* (as trodden); figuratively a *course* of life or *mode* of action:— along, away, custom, journey, manner, through, toward, way, highway, pathway, withersoever

G390 *anastrephō*; to *overturn*; also to *return*; by implication to *busy oneself*; i.e. *remain, live*:— abide, behave self, be used, overthrow, pass, return

G391 *anastrophē* from G390; *behavior*:— conversation

G5158 *tropos*; a *turn*, i.e. (by implication) *mode* or *style*, figuratively *deportment* or *character*:— (like) manner, (by any) means, way

G4176 *politeuomai*; to *behave* as a citizen (figuratively):— let conversation be, live

G4175 *politeuma* from G4176; a *community*, i.e. (abstractly) *citizenship*:— conversation

Psalm 37:14 and 50:23 are the only places where the "trodden road" definition of conversation (H1870) is found. Imagine your life is one long road, and every day is another step forward in your journey. There are side trails and lookout points, even places to stop and rest, but you get to choose how to traverse this course. There are consequences for the steps you take; not all paths are right and true. Herein lies the call to "order our conversation aright," to rightly choose the correct path and walk in it, not allowing fear or laziness or inner defiance to deviate from it.

Wherein in time past ye walked according to the course of this world, according to the prince of the power of the air, the spirit that now worketh in the children of disobedience:
Among whom also we all had our conversation in times past in the lust of the flesh, fulfilling the desires of the flesh and of the mind; and were by nature the children of wrath, even as others. (Ephesians 2:2–3)

In the Ephesians verses above, as well as in Ephesians 4:22, 2 Corinthians 1:12, and Galatians 1:13, Paul called on his brethren to no longer live (or have their *conversation*, G390) by the old ways. He wanted them to remember how they used to behave and to refuse to go back to living like that again. Ephesians 2:3 declares that we all lived by the lust of the flesh and were by nature the children of wrath. It's discomfiting to think how worldly we were. How our whole lives were consumed by selfish pursuits. How we busied ourselves with what pleased us. This was our "conversation in times past." But thanks be to God who is rich in mercy, He has turned us around from that destructive path. And because we reversed our course and overturned the reign of self by the power of His Spirit, we are no longer called the children of wrath.

> *Let no man despise thy youth; but be thou an example of the believers, in word, in conversation, in charity, in spirit, in purity. (1 Timothy 4:12)*

Paul told Timothy how to conduct himself as a minister of God. Being an example "in conversation" (G391) simply meant how he chose to present his overall behavior. Although we women are not pastors, Paul's words apply to us too. We need to be an example to our fellow sisters not only in what we say but in how we live.

> *Remember them which have the rule over you, who have spoken unto you the word of God: whose faith follow, considering the end of their conversation. (Hebrews 13:7)*

Hebrews 13:7 is on the recipient side of what Paul told Timothy. Those faithful ministers and pastors who oversee the flock of God, who spend their lives for the benefit of others need our respect. This verse in Hebrews can also apply to faithful husbands who guide their families. The "end of their conversation" is the result of the way they live, the fruit they produce by abiding in Christ.

In 1 Peter 3:2, the apostle Peter explained to believing wives that their behavior, their "chaste conversation coupled with fear," would be the swaying factor for their unbelieving husbands to consider and yield to the truth of God's Word.

> *Likewise, ye wives, be in subjection to your own husbands; that, if any obey not the word, they also may without the word be won by the conversation of the wives. (1 Peter 3:1)*

It is our pure and faithful lives in Christ that will make the difference for our men and not the many words, debates, and arguments for Christ we could wield.

Unbelievers, called *Gentiles* in the KJV, may speak maliciously against us as 1 Peter 2:12 says they will, but they won't be able to deny the good works they witness through our honest behavior, and some will even glorify God (because of our positive influence, perhaps?) upon His return. Speaking of Christ's return:

> *But the day of the Lord will come as a thief in the night; in the which the heavens shall pass away with a great noise, and the elements shall melt with fervent heat, the earth also and the works that are therein shall be burned up.*
>
> *Seeing then that all these things shall be dissolved, what manner of persons ought ye to be in all holy conversation and godliness. (2 Peter 3:10–11)*

How we women conduct ourselves is of utmost importance. The world is watching, our spouses are watching, our children are watching and learning. And every physical thing we've worked so hard for in this temporal world will be gone. The only thing left, the only thing to show for our time here, will be our Christian character.

Researching the word *conversation* in the context of Philippians 3:20 reveals so much about the purpose for our lives that God, in His love, has made possible. Conversation (G4175) translates to *citizenship*.

> *For our conversation is in heaven; from whence also we look for the Savior, the Lord Jesus Christ. (Philippians 3:20)*

Our citizenship or community is at the throne of God! He has made us a part of His family, and when Christ returns, He brings with Him our citizenship papers that usher us into His glorious millennial kingdom.

> *Only let your conversation be as it becomes the gospel of Christ . . . that ye stand fast in one spirit, with one mind striving together for the faith of the gospel. (Philippians 1:27)*

Paul urged the brethren at Philippi to *behave as citizens* of the gospel (G4176), to live as a representative of the gospel of Christ. We, as ambassadors of Christ, as daughters of the King, show through our words and deeds the hope and love that dwells in Him.

Let your conversation be without covetousness;
and be content with such things as ye have: for he
hath said, I will never leave thee, nor forsake thee.
(Hebrews 13:5)

Let your conversation, dear women—the way you live, your demeanor, your manner of conducting and bearing yourself—be without a constant desire for more. The world says we need to be prettier, thinner, and more talented. The world says we need more stuff in our homes, more money in our bank accounts, and more clothes in our closets. But God knows our true needs. He will never leave our side. He has said it and cannot lie. His unfathomable love, the characteristic *conversation* of God, can be counted on.

Who is a wise man and endued with knowledge
among you? let him shew out of a good conversation
his works with meekness of wisdom. (James 3:13)

Edify

*Wherefore comfort yourselves together, and **edify** one another, even as you do. (1 Thessalonians 5:11)*

Did you know you were a carpenter? Yes, every time you encourage someone to press on despite their pain, or you lift their burdens in prayer, a doorway is made, a window is cut, and a room is laid out. When we edify, we swing mighty hammers of love, and our plumb lines point straight to God's truth. A magnificent building is rising off the foundation of our stalwart Cornerstone—Jesus Christ.

Seeking comfort in our common misery is normal. But if someone simply commiserates with our plight, how would that help us, truly? Godly comfort is more than acknowledging the pain of our dear sisters; it is leading them away from despair by reminding them of their hope in Christ. It is emboldening them to overcome doubts and strengthen their wobbly legs in courage. This comfort builds. This comfort *edifies*.

Edify

G3619 *oikodomē*; *architecture*, (concretely) a *structure*; figuratively *confirmation*:— building

G3618 *oikodomeō*; to be a *house-builder*, *construct* or (figuratively) *confirm*:— build (up), (be in) building up, embolden

Edification G3619: see definition above

Edified G3618: see definition above

Edifieth G3618: see definition above

Edifying G3619: see definition above

G3622 *oikonomia*; *administration* (over a household or estate), specifically a (religious) *"economy"*:— dispensation, stewardship

To edify (*oikodomeō*, G3618) is to be a house builder. How awesome to think we've been given this capability! Our brothers and sisters are part of the house of God, and we can aid in their spiritual growth and development by our Spirit-led words and actions. "Let every one of us please his neighbour for his good to edification" (Romans 15:2). Yet, as with any responsibility, our intention must always be for the good of the other. We may have great gifts (speaking, writing, teaching), but if they aren't geared toward building up our fellow sisters, we only have the sounding brass and tinkling cymbal of self-promotion. "For thou givest thanks well, but the other is not edified" (1 Corinthians 14:17). Paul cautioned against the pride of our abilities, specifically the use of speaking in tongues (foreign languages).

> *He that speaketh in an unknown tongue edifieth himself; but he that prophesieth edifieth the church. (1 Corinthians 14:4)*

Just like the early church's gift of tongues, our personal biblical knowledge can be a hindrance to someone else's growth if we don't wield it with gentle, godly love.

> *Now as touching things offered unto idols, we know that we all have knowledge. Knowledge puffeth up, but charity edifieth. (1 Corinthians 8:10)*

Truth is truth. But everyone on this Christian path is given knowledge at a pace befitting that individual. God knows our spiritual frames. He knows when we are ready

for the next layers of brick and mortar. Speaking the truth
in love is key to the proper building up of the sound
structure of our spiritual family.

> *Let us therefore follow after the things that make for*
> *peace, and things wherewith one may edify another.*
> *(Romans 14:19)*

> *But speaking the truth in love, may* [we, the
> church] *grow up into him in all things, which is the*
> *head, even Christ:*
> *From whom the whole body fitly joined together*
> *and compacted by that which every joint supplieth,*
> *according to the effectual working in the measure of*
> *every part, maketh increase of the body unto the*
> *edifying of itself in love. (Ephesians 4:15–16)*

With any building addition or remodeling project, you
will inevitably have to tear down crumbling walls, reinforce
beams and openings, and remove unsightly or unnecessary
sections before the beauty of a sound structure is revealed.
The renovation of our hearts is no different. It hurts. We
must be willing to dismantle the façade of fear, tear down
the partitions of sin—those false panels we think are not
there—and scrape off the peeling paint of self-righteousness.
If we don't, this house of our own making will stifle our
spiritual growth and grieve the Spirit of God.

Once we yield, however, it will be easier to recognize
the same marred framework in our sisters. And because we
don't want to see their houses fall, we have a responsibility

to say something, as painful for us or as "destructive" for them as it may feel at the time, to remind them of their true calling as women of God. We edify when we speak the truth in love.

Therefore I write these things being absent, lest being present I should use sharpness, according to the power which the Lord hath given me to edification, and not to destruction. (2 Corinthians 13:10)

And of some have compassion, making a difference: And others save with fear, pulling them out of the fire; hating even the garment spotted by the flesh. (Jude 22–23)

Edifying can take many forms. From the resolute whisper of consolation to the clarion call to wake up. But whichever is used, our motivation should always be for the spiritual building up of the other and not the prideful tearing down.

Again, think ye that we excuse ourselves unto you? we speak before God in Christ: but we do all things, dearly beloved, for your edifying. (2 Corinthians 12:19)

The noun form of edify is *edification* (G3619), which means "confirmation," or making firm, establishing, and strengthening the soundness of a structure, whether it be a home, a family, a church, or an individual.

> *Know ye not that ye are the temple of God, and*
> *that the Spirit of God dwelleth in you?*
> *(1 Corinthians 3:16)*

Will this structure hold up under tremendous pressure? Is it strong enough to withstand the fiercest storm? We ask these questions of our physical dwellings, but what about our spiritual ones? What about our family relationships and communities? If the power of Christ lives within us, the answer is a resounding yes! God has given each of us certain house-building gifts. What is yours? Teaching, hospitality, speaking words of encouragement or discernment, or ministering to the needs of others? Whatever it is, use it:

> *For the perfecting of the saints, for the work of the*
> *ministry, for the edifying of the body of Christ:*
> *Till we all come in the unity of the faith, and of the*
> *knowledge of the Son of God, into a perfect man, of*
> *the stature of the fulness of Christ.*
> *(Ephesians 4:12–13)*

House building takes work. But as we continue swinging those hammers and sweeping those floors, our reward will be an eternal edifice of grandeur.

> *Ye also, as lively stones, are built up a spiritual house,*
> *an holy priesthood, to offer up spiritual sacrifices,*
> *acceptable to God by Jesus Christ. (1 Peter 2:5)*

May our concrete foundation be the bedrock
  of Truth,
Framed with the steel studs of faith
  that neither bend nor break.
Walls wrapped in the lath and plaster
  of the knowledge of God.
Mercy and forgiveness wired throughout.
Windows reflecting the image of Christ.
A gilded building,
  a spiritual house.
Painted with peace
  and trimmed with joy.
Sealed with the lacquer of love.

[6]

Ensue/Eschew

*Let him **eschew** evil, and do good; let him seek peace, and
ensue it. (1 Peter 3:11)*

The definition of ensue, which you've probably already
guessed from the verse above, is to "pursue," or to
"follow after." Both ensue and pursue come from the same
Greek word *diō* meaning to "flee." What you probably
didn't know is the word *ensue* has the same meaning as the
word *persecute* in the KJV.

On the other side of our word study is *eschew*, a
funny-sounding word like someone sneezed. To eschew
is to "shun or avoid something." This is the see-saw to
ensue—the opposite admonition, more or less, of pursuing
something. There is only one instance of ensue and one
of eschew in the New Testament. Be prepared to fall into
joyful rabbit holes that reveal rich layers of spiritual
insight as we research these two words.

Ensue

G1377 *diōkō*; to *pursue* (literally or figuratively); by implication to *persecute*:— follow (after), given to, (suffer) persecution, persecution, press forward

Eschew

G1578 *ekklinō*; to *deviate* (absolutely) to *shun* (literally or figuratively), or to *decline* (from piety):— avoid, go out of the way

Eschewed H5493 *sûr*; to *turn off* (literally or figuratively):— call back, decline, depart, leave undone, pluck away, put away, rebel, remove, revolt, take away, turn away, be without

Escheweth H5493: see definition above

King David's words from the Psalms and Peter's in the book of 1 Peter are almost identical side-by-side.

Depart from evil, and do good; seek peace, and pursue it. (Psalm 34:14)	*Let him eschew evil, and do good; let him seek peace, and ensue it. (1 Peter 3:11)*

The Hebrew definition of pursue (H7291 to *run after, chase, put to flight, hunt, persecute*) usually means to go after something with hostile intent, but in 1 Peter, the word *ensue* encourages us to pursue peace with dogged determination, something we don't let up on. But as we ensue or follow after peace determinedly, the very definition of ensue suggests we may suffer persecution for it. Why is that and from whom?

In this life, to wholeheartedly follow after the peace God gives is not easy. What is easy is to let frenzied emotions and bad attitudes take hold of us when things go wrong. People won't understand our calm demeanor and meek and quiet spirit—which in the sight of God is of great price (1 Peter 3:4)—if we don't react the way they would. Their response to us might be chiding and ridicule. Remember Job's wife (Job 2:9)?

What is this peace we are to follow hard after? When we think of peace, we think of not having to deal with our cranky toddler, demanding spouse, or overbearing in-laws. Our notion of peace is a convenience for ourselves where our comfort zone is not invaded, and where we're blissfully left alone. There is nothing wrong with a cozy blanket, a warm cup of tea, a quiet room and a book, and no demands for the moment. But life in this world cannot sustain that kind of peace. That is why we need Christ's.

Peace I leave with you, my peace I give unto you: not as the world giveth, give I unto you. Let not your heart be troubled, neither let it be afraid. (John 14:27)

The peace Christ spoke of means to *join*; by implication *prosperity*. Peace (G1515) in the KJV means "one, quietness, rest, set at one again." Prosperity, quietness, and rest. These three things sound quite peaceful, don't they? But what does to "join," "one," or "set at one" have to do with peace? These phrases point back to who God is and what His purpose for us has been from the beginning—to become one with Him and His Son, Jesus Christ. "I and my Father are one" (John 10:30).

And the glory which thou gavest me I have given them; that they may be one, even as we are one. I in them, and thou in me, that they may be made perfect in one; and that the world may know that thou hast sent me, and hast loved them, as thou hast loved me. (John 17:22–23)

Paul urged us several times in the book of Philippians to be one with each other, to mind the same things, and to be of one mind with our fellow believers. Like a husband and wife are one, peacefulness is the result of joining:

become one with God, with your husband, and with your fellow believers.

But what if your computer dies, you lose your job, your house floods, your health fails, your country succumbs to communism? So many things can go wrong to disturb you and cause you grief. How do you "ensue" peace as the apostle Peter taught? Where do you find Christ's peace in these situations? And what exactly is Christ's peace? His peace is your ability, however imperfectly done, to accept misfortune and upheaval in your life and still breathe steadily without stress, knowing God is in control of every detail of your life. The circumstances and stressors still exist, but Christ covers them, separates them from affecting your spirit negatively. Like He said in John 16:33, "I have overcome the world"! How else can poverty-stricken, war-torn, perse-cuted Christians around the world smile, laugh, and find joy while misery abounds? They must, like we, ensue peace.

What was the first thing Jesus Christ told His disciples after his ascension? "Peace be unto you." That's what He wants for all of us. Supernatural peace that transcends our earth-bound understanding (Philippians 4:7).

Let us therefore follow after the things that make for peace, and things wherewith one may edify another. (Romans 14:19)

When we look closely at Romans 14:19, we discover that the phrase "follow after" (*diōkō*, G1377) is the same word for *ensue*. But what things "make for peace"? If we pursue peace, if we pursue what makes for peace, we must actively live by God's love. If we pursue godly love, peace will naturally follow because they're connected. It's divine symbiosis. Isn't it ironic that our initial, purely selfish desire for peace requires an unselfish surrender to live by God's love before we can find it? You can't have peace without living by love. The more we love others like Christ loves us, the more His peace settles upon us.

The word *eschew* is found four times in the KJV. All three Old Testament instances of the word are found in the book of Job paired with the phrase "one that feared God."

> *There was a man in the land of Uz, whose name was Job; and that man was perfect and upright, and one that feared God, and eschewed evil. (Job 1:1)*

Job didn't merely turn away from evil, he first feared God. He regarded God in the most highly esteemed way not wanting any possibility of offending Him or sinning against Him. Job offered God burnt offerings for his grown children *just in case* they might have sinned in their hearts. He understood who God is: righteous, holy, and worthy of praise. Job feared and took seriously the God of the universe and the giver of life and actively turned away from any appearance of evil (Ephesians 5:11).

> *Let him eschew evil, and do good; let him seek peace, and ensue it. (1 Peter 3:11)*

To eschew is to *shun*, *turn your back* on something, and run from it. When we think of pure evil—ugly, dreadful, frightful evil—the first impulse we have is to quickly turn the other way. We know it comes directly from Satan and his demons and want nothing of it. But often we don't realize we harbor evil thoughts, evil intentions, evil deeds in our lives. Rage, doubt, impatience, disrespect, stubbornness, pride. These are all evil, the opposite of God's character. Everyone has lived out these characteristics at one time or another. The key here is do we see the dreadful ugliness in them? Do we ask God to rout these sins inside us? Or do we gloss over these traits believing they're not that bad? The world wants us to embrace "our true selves" and revel in that, certainly not conform to who God is.

First Samuel 15:23 is an eye-opener. "For rebellion is as the sin of witchcraft, and stubbornness is as iniquity and idolatry." Wow! We know that witchcraft is evil and would never engage in it. And we know idolatry is evil and wouldn't take part in that either. But in 1 Samuel, these two evil practices are equated with rebellion and stubbornness. Two actions every one of us has taken part in and might still be doing without realizing it.

- ❀ Do we refuse to give God our full submission, holding back a part of ourselves?
- ❀ Do we ignore certain parts of God's Word because it makes us feel uncomfortable?
- ❀ Do we doubt God will care for us during our worst times and indulge in worrying over our trying circumstances? "Take heed, brethren, lest there be in any of you an evil heart of unbelief, in departing from the living God" (Hebrews 3:12).

Rebellion and stubbornness are evils we should eschew as quickly as if we walked into an ominous and begrimed alley at midnight alone.

Romans 12:18 tells us, if it is possible, to live peaceably with all men. But sometimes it isn't possible. To live by the love of God and live in peace sometimes require drastic measures. If we are to eschew evil (anything contrary to God's Word) and seek peace and pursue it, we may have to change who we associate with. For the sake of peace and our own spiritual integrity, we may need to cut all ties with certain family members and friends (Romans 16:17–18). God wants us to live in peace, but not at the expense of our faith. If we accept the watering down of God's Word by others (especially those who call themselves Christians) so we won't have to deal with the emotional conflict our speaking up may cause, this is merely a false peace and puts us in dangerous waters.

True godly peace is not a big group-hug moment of toleration. "Can't we all just get along?" is not the answer and will not usher in peace. Getting along with the world's ideology of anything goes for the sake of peace makes you a partaker of their evil deeds even if you don't do the same things. You forfeit your child-of-God status for a few social invitations, phone calls, pats on the back, and smiling clan photos that amount to nothing on the scale of eternity.

Although eschew is only found three times in the Old Testament, the word *depart* (H5493) is found numerous times and is derived from the same Hebrew word *sûr* that eschew is derived from. In its simplest form, the Bible teaches us to turn away from evil in all its forms and follow after good things:

righteousness, faith, love, and peace. It's a life-long pursuit to live holy. And the reward is peace in the presence of God forevermore.

> *Depart from evil, and do good; and dwell for evermore. For the Lord loveth judgment, and forsaketh not his saints; they are preserved for ever: but the seed of the wicked shall be cut off. (Psalm 37:27–28)*

[7]

Exhort

*But **exhort** one another daily, while it is called To Day; lest any of you be hardened through the deceitfulness of sin. (Hebrews 3:13)*

Bound together by faith in Christ, another one of our Christian duties is exhortation. When you exhort others, you comfort, encourage, plead, and advise them to follow a better way. You hand them a royal invitation embossed with love and life-giving words you hope they will accept.

- ❀ "Stand strong in the faith, my friend. Don't give up!"
- ❀ "Be careful who and what you listen to. Don't be fooled."
- ❀ "Life is hard, I know, but you'll get through this with God's help. He has promised!"
- ❀ "God will never leave you nor forsake you; believe that, my dear."

Exhort

G3870 *parakaleō*; to *call near, invite, invoke* (by *imploration, exhortation,* or *consolation*):— beseech, call for, (be of good) comfort, desire, (give) exhortation, entreat, pray

G3867 *paraineō*; to *mispraise,* to *recommend* or *advise* (a different course):— admonish

Exhortation G3870: see definition above

G3874 *paraklēsis* from G3870; *imploration, exhortation, solace*:— comfort, consolation, entreaty

G3056 logos; something *said* (including the *thought*); by implication a *topic* (subject of discourse), also *reasoning* (the mental faculty), or *motive*:— account, cause, communication, doctrine, matter

Exhorted G3870: see definition above

Exhorteth G3870: see definition above

Exhorting G3870: see definition above

G4389 *protrepomai*; to *turn forward* for oneself, *encourage*:— exhort

Exhortation (calling forth, inviting) is akin to *admonishing* (warning) and *beseeching* (pleading). All three words are used—sometimes interchangeably—in the KJV for getting someone's attention. But one thing is clear: when we exhort, our invitation should be for the love of the one spoken to and not for selfish or prideful means.

> *For our exhortation was not of deceit, nor of uncleanness, nor in guile:*
> *But as we were allowed of God to be put in trust with the gospel, even so we speak; not as pleasing men, but God, which trieth our hearts.*
> *(1 Thessalonians 2:3–4)*

Exhortation is not only a heartfelt petition to inspire others to hear words of wisdom but also a gift of the Spirit. Have you been given this gift?

> *Having then gifts differing according to the grace that is given to us, whether prophecy, let us prophesy according to the proportion of faith;*
> *Or ministry, let us wait on our ministering: or he that teacheth, on teaching;*
> *Or he that exhorteth, on exhortation: he that giveth, let him do it with simplicity; he that ruleth, with diligence; he that sheweth mercy, with cheerfulness.*
> *(Romans 12:6–8)*

Every Christian is required to love the brethren by warning, comforting, and supporting them as spoken of in

Hebrews 3:13, but God may have given you a stronger propensity to excel at exhortation. If so, you've been given a blessed gift of counsel where your well-timed words become the motivating factor someone needs to bolster their faith or lean hard upon during moments of wavering, weariness, and desperation. When you exhort someone, you do a myriad of things depending on the situation:

- ❀ Console someone over a loss and give them hope
- ❀ Bring to their attention an error in theological understanding with humility
- ❀ Encourage them to press on despite the many obstacles in their life
- ❀ Shake them out of their spiritual complacency with loving words of warning

No matter what form our exhortation takes, we are called to exhort our brothers and sisters in Christ daily because everyone has low points and hard days and needs to be held accountable, encouraged, and kept steadily on the right path.

> *Now we exhort you, brethren, warn them that are unruly, comfort the feebleminded, support the weak, be patient toward all men.*
> *See that none render evil for evil unto any man; but ever follow that which is good, both among yourselves, and to all men.*
> *(1 Thessalonians 5:14–15)*

These bidding words of ours could be the very words someone needs at a pivotal moment in their faith journey. But the matter always falls on the hearer to heed. Our duty is to speak, but it's up to them to follow through.

In Acts chapter 2, Peter spoke boldly to those who would listen in Jerusalem to repent of their sins and turn to God, exhorting them that if they would be baptized in the name of Jesus Christ, they would receive the gift of the Holy Spirit. "And with many other words did he testify and exhort, saying, Save yourselves from this untoward generation" (Acts 2:40). Paul and Barnabas had their own commission to share the good news with the Gentiles, but it was not without trial and danger.

> *And when they had preached the gospel to that city, and had taught many, they returned again to Lystra, and to Iconium, and Antioch,*
> *Confirming the souls of the disciples, and exhorting them to continue in the faith, and that we must through much tribulation enter into the kingdom of God. (Acts 14:21–22)*

Jude is known for his no-holds-barred approach to speaking the truth in his one-chapter letter. Through mighty exhortation, he pleads with the beloved brethren to "earnestly contend for the faith," and to continue living that truth in unabashed strength (Jude 3).

Like Jude, we not only care deeply for our fellow Christians, but also for our families and close friends (Christian or not), and when we teach our children or

converse with friends, we want them to hear us. We want
them to steer clear of the easy road with its false promises
and stay on the path of life. But if they refuse to listen, it
causes us great pain because we know by experience what
refusal does to the soul. The apostles had the same desire
and conflict.

> *As ye know how we exhorted and comforted and
> charged every one of you, as a father doth his
> children. (1 Thessalonians 2:11)*

> *And ye have forgotten the exhortation which
> speaketh unto you as unto children, My son, despise
> not thou the chastening of the Lord, nor faint when
> thou art rebuked of him. (Hebrews 12:5)*

> *And I beseech you, brethren, suffer the word of
> exhortation: for I have written a letter unto you in
> few words. (Hebrews 13:22)*

Have you ever bristled with pride when a fellow
believer or even your spouse called you out on an error?
The book of Hebrews teaches us to "suffer the word" or *put
up with* or *bear with* the truth that others speak for our own
good. Whenever we're on the receiving end of exhortation, let us not allow our feelings to create a barrier to this
God-inspired help. Painful as it may be, let us not hold on
to offense that would cause us to delay (or worse, diminish)
our growth in Christ.

Furthermore then we beseech you, brethren, and exhort you by the Lord Jesus, that as ye have received of us how ye ought to walk and to please God, so ye would abound more and more.
(1 Thessalonians 4:1)

The apostle Paul loved Timothy like a dear son. In his absence, Paul wanted Timothy to grow and excel in the faith. Christ desires this very thing for us. Let us accept Paul's invitation to Timothy as if it were handed directly by Christ to us. "Till I come, give attendance to reading, to exhortation, to doctrine" (1 Timothy 4:13). While you wait for Christ's return, stay in the Word of God. By doing so, your exhortations will be based on sound teachings and make a positive spiritual impact on your family, friends, and fellow sisters in Christ.

Holding fast the faithful word as he hath been taught, that he may be able by sound doctrine both to exhort and to convince the gainsayers. (Titus 1:9)

Meet

*We are bound to thank God always for you, brethren, as it is **meet**, because that your faith groweth exceedingly.*
(2 Thessalonians 1:3)

A nib of a pen gliding on paper. A key that fits perfectly into its lock. Lenses that bring what is blurred into focus. Spiritual truth delivering hope. The one is meant for the other, you see. It is needful. It is necessary. It is meet.

The word *meet* used in the KJV does not always mean what we expect it to mean as a verb: to join up with someone, or to encounter something; or as a noun: an assembly of some kind. "There is that scattereth, and yet increaseth; and there is that withholdeth more than is meet, but tendeth to poverty" (Proverbs 11:24). Here in Proverbs, meet is not a verb, nor is it a noun, but an adjective. Meet describes how and in what way something *is*. There are those who give and give without fear of loss and continue to have more to give because of it, and then there are those

Meet

H5828 *ēzer*; *aid*:— help

H3476 *yōšer* taken from H3474; the *right*:— equity, right, upright, uprightness

H3477 *yāšār* taken from H3474; *straight* (literally or figuratively):— convenient, equity, just, pleased well, right, righteous, upright

H3474 *yāšar*; to be *straight* or *even*; to be (or *make*) *right*, *pleasant*, *prosperous*:— direct, fit, seem good, please well, esteem right, make straight

G514 *axios*; *deserving*, *comparable* or *suitable* (as if *drawing* praise):— due reward, worthy, unworthy

G2570 *kalos*; *beautiful*, but chiefly (figuratively) *good* (literally or morally) i.e. *valuable* or *virtuous* (for *appearance* or *use*):— better, fair, good, goodly, honest, well, worthy [Matthew 15:26; Mark 7:26]

G1163 *dei* also *deon* both used impersonally; *it is* (*was*) necessary (as *binding*):— behoved, must (needs), need, be needful, ought, should

G1342 *dikaios*; *equitable* (in character or act), by implication *innocent*, *holy*:— just, right, righteous

G2427 *hikanoō*; to *enable*, i.e. *qualify*:— make able

G2173 *euchrēstos*; *easily used*, i.e. *useful*:— profitable, meet for use

G2111 *euthetos*; *well placed*, i.e. (figuratively) *appropriate*:— fit

There are several more entries for the word *meet* in noun, verb, and adjectival forms, but only numbered entries with Bible verse examples are listed here.

who hold back more than is *meet* (H3476), or more than is "right, equitable, and necessary" and suffer greater loss because of it.

> *We are bound to thank God always for you, brethren, as it is meet, because that your faith groweth exceedingly. (2 Thessalonians 1:3)*

> *It was meet that we should make merry, and be glad: for this thy brother was dead, and is alive again; and was lost, and is found. (Luke 15:32)*

It is especially meet (G514) or "rewarding" or "suitable" to see spiritual growth in our fellow brethren. And when a family member chooses to walk in truth, there is no greater joy! Although we may be knit together by blood, it is the bond of the Spirit that makes us kin.

"Yea, I think it meet, as long as I am in this tabernacle, to stir you up by putting you in remembrance" (2 Peter 1:13). It was meet (G1342) or "right judgment" for Peter, as long as he lived, to keep the works of faith in the forefront of the believers' minds. It is right judgment for us to do the same. When we add virtue, knowledge, self-control, patience, godliness, brotherly kindness, and love to our faith, and spur others on to do the same, we are assured we will never be barren or unfruitful in the knowledge of our Lord Jesus Christ (2 Peter 1:5–7).

John the Baptist dared warn the Sadducees and Pharisees (those who thought themselves pleasing to God because of their heritage and place in society) of their arrogance:

> *Bring therefore fruits meet for repentance:*
> *And think not to say within yourselves, We have*
> *Abraham to our father: for I say unto you, that*
> *God is able of these stones to raise up children*
> *unto Abraham.*
> *And now also the axe is laid unto the root of the*
> *trees: therefore every tree which bringeth not forth*
> *good fruit is hewn down, and cast into the fire.*
> *(Matthew 3:8–10)*

God's truth either compels someone to change or offends them. Paul spoke to the Jews in Acts 26:20 and told them they ought to repent and turn to God and do works meet for repentance, and they nearly killed him for it. The indignation others feel, the offense to Christ they harbor, may not result in your physical harm, as it does with brethren in other parts of the world, but in your being mocked at work, shadowbanned on social media, or shunned by family members. When we humbly offer fruits worthy of repentance, our Father makes us worthy partakers of His coming kingdom, a far better trade-off than friendship with the world.

> *Giving thanks unto the Father, which hath made us*
> *meet to be partakers of the inheritance of the saints*
> *in light:*
> *Who hath delivered us from the power of darkness,*
> *and hath translated us into the kingdom of his dear*
> *Son. (Colossians 1:12–13)*

We have been delivered from the power of darkness, praise God, but we still suffer on this earth as His children. Our trials of lack and loss serve a glorious purpose hard to comprehend while living through them. But they are meet (G2111 *useful*, *well placed*, and *necessary*) for our spiritual growth. Every time you allow patience to reign over your spirit of complaint, every time you shout no to the adversary's whispers to give in, every time you choose to love when anger or laziness is your first response, you become meet for the Master's use and prepared for every good work (2 Timothy 2:21). Like rain falling long on the desert floor, the knowledge of Jesus Christ soaks into your parched and weary heart and provides you with everything you need to blossom in life and godliness.

I have made the earth, the man and the beast that are upon the ground, by my great power and by my outstretched arm, and have given it unto whom it seemed meet unto me. (Jeremiah 27:5)

God has made what He has for whom He has according to His good pleasure. It seemed meet (H3474), or "good, well-pleasing, and right," to God to bless us with His creation. The most remarkable of His creations was the female human being. She was unique in that God could have created her right along with Adam, as He did the animals (Genesis 2:20). But He didn't. He chose to let Adam feel something amiss in his nascent life. He chose to allow Adam a time of loneliness to realize his great need for a companion.

And the Lord God said, It is not good that the man
should be alone; I will make him an help meet for
him. (Genesis 2:18)

For the first time in all His creation, God pronounced
something **not** good. Man was not meant to be alone.
Woman would be the embodiment of the perfect mate:
lover, partner, supporter, and friend. She would aid him in
all he set his hands to do. She would, according to God
Himself, be "an help meet," a help suitable for the man He
just breathed life into.

There's nothing more fulfilling—nor exhausting!—
than being a proper helpmeet for your husband. When
you think of the phrase "help meet" from the Bible, your
first thought might be that both words combine to make
a noun like they do in *Merriam-Webster's Collegiate
Dictionary*. But the reality is that "help" is a noun (it's what
you are) *and* a verb (it's what you do) and "meet" is an
adjective describing how and in what way you are a help
to your husband. When you are a help *meet*, you are a
help *suitable* for the man God gave you.

Second Timothy 2:21 tells us that we are vessels meet
for the Master's use if we depart from iniquity and do good
works. To God, we are suitable for our calling, valuable in
His eyes, well-placed in His family, useful for encouraging
our fellow brethren, and just and holy as long as we stay in
His hands. When you embody your role as a helpmeet for
your husband, you become a useful aid, a beautiful
assistant, a necessary helper, a just and holy well-placed
companion who surrounds, relieves, and supports her man.

God created the epitome of what a man needed in a woman:

- ❀ She would surround him with love and laughter.
- ❀ She would be worthy of his trust and affection.
- ❀ She would protect his heart and give him a purpose for living.

She is the perfect gift. Woman is meant for Man, you see. She is needful. She is necessary. She is meet.

As for me, behold, I am in your hand: do with me as seemeth good and meet unto you. (Jeremiah 26:14)

[9]

Nought

*And he answered and told them, "Elias verily cometh first, and restoreth all things; and how it is written of the Son of man, that he must suffer many things, and be set at **nought**." (Mark 9:12)*

N ought is a word we ought not mistake for a mere variant spelling of the word *naught*, meaning "nothing" as *Merriam-Webster's Dictionary* defines it. The KJV includes both words, *nought* and *naught*, but each has separate and varied meanings. Although nought usually means "not any" or "nothing," more is being said in the phrase "set at nought" in Mark 9 above and in Acts 4:11 about our lord, Jesus Christ.

> *This is the stone which was set at nought of you builders, which is become the head of the corner. (Acts 4:11).*

Nought

H2600 *ḥinnān; gratis*, i.e. devoid of cost, reason, or advantage:— without a cause, without a cost, for nothing, in vain

H8045 *šāmad;* to desolate:— destroy, destruction, bring to nought, overthrow, perish, pluck down, utterly

H6565 *pārar;* to *break* up (figuratively, i.e. to *violate, frustrate*):— break asunder, cast off, cause to cease, defeat, disappoint, dissolve, divide, make of none effect, fail, make void

H369 *ayin;* from a primitive root meaning to *be nothing* or *not exist; a non-entity*:— fail, fatherless, be gone, incurable, none, not, unsearchable, without

H6331 *pûr;* to *crush*:— break, utterly take

H8414 *tōhû* from an unused root meaning to lie *waste;* a *desolation* (of surface), i.e. *desert;* figuratively a *worthless* thing; adverbially in *vain*:— confusion, empty place, without form, nothing, vain, vanity, wilderness

H656 *āpēs;* to *disappear*, i.e. *cease*:— be clean gone, be at an end, be brought to nought, fail

H657 *epes* from H656; *cessation*, i.e. an *end* (especially of the earth); *no further*:— howbeit, less than nothing, notwithstanding, thing of nought

H434 *ĕlûl;* good for *nothing*:— thing of nought

G1847 *exoudenoō;* to *make utterly nothing of*, i.e. *despise*:— set at nought

G1848 *exoutheneō;* meaning the same as G1847:— contemptible, despise, least esteemed

G2673 *katargeō;* to be (render) entirely idle (useless):— abolish, cease, destroy, do away, become of no effect, fail, vanish away, make void

Naught H7451 *ra*; *bad* or (as noun) *evil* (natural or moral):— adversity, affliction, bad, calamity, grief, harm, heavy, hurt, ill (favoured), mischief, misery, sore, sorrow, trouble, vex, wicked, worse, wretchedness, wrong

Due to the multitude of definition entries for *nought*, only entries with Bible verse examples in this chapter are listed in the chart.

The savior of all mankind, the Son of man, who came to set aright our standing with the Father, was made utterly nothing of by the world He created. He was despised and lightly esteemed by the religious leaders of His day and the nation He was born into.

In Romans 14:10, Paul warned us not to "set at nought" or despise and look down upon our brothers and sisters in Christ for what we may consider a weak application of their faith regarding non-salvation issues. They stand or fall to their own Master, according to their own conscience, as do we. Their knowledge of God will change over time as they mature in Christ. With Christianity, we don't end in the same place we start. At least we shouldn't. God is gracious to us in our wobbly starts, and so must we be to others.

The Christian faith is fraught with weariness of spirit. When we don't see immediate results in our ministries, in our personal disciplines of patience, hospitality, forgiveness, and long-suffering, our tenacious godly work can seem like wasted effort. We feel like the good we do is for nothing. Is our service to God for nought (H2600 *without a cause, for nothing, in vain*)? Our heads know this is false, but our hearts sometimes wonder. And we wouldn't be the first to feel so.

> *Then I said, I have laboured in vain, I have spent my strength for nought, and in vain: yet surely my judgment is with the Lord, and my work with my God. (Isaiah 49:4)*

Adult children or friends who've rebelled against God weigh heavy on our hearts, and no amount of pleading with them or desperate prayers has done any good. Marriage woes and our own stubborn sins that anger and frustrate us still cling like the tentacles of an alien beast. We want change to happen right away, our efforts to pay off, yet they come to nought. Or so they seem. God is not pressured by time like we are. He knows the end from the beginning, from ancient times to times yet fulfilled (Isaiah 46:10). He has patience for the harvest, unlike us. That is why we are encouraged to continue doing the right thing, for in due time—God's time—our faithful toil will be rewarded. (See 1 Corinthians 15:58; Galatians 6:9.)

Even with earthly desires, we set our hearts on dreams and ideas, hopes for beauty and prosperity that never succeed. A new car to replace that clunker in the driveway, a spacious pretty home instead of the one you wake up to, a flourishing business that reflects your talents and lifts your family's financial burdens. We pursue these dreams like we see others do, but ours come to nought (H6565 *cause to cease, disappoint, break up, dissolve*). Although these dreams of ours aren't bad, God intervened and said no. They came to nought because their success would have distracted us and hampered our spiritual growth. And God loves us too much for that.

Speaking of what is or isn't bad, the word *naught* (H7451) in the KJV means exactly that: bad, evil, wicked. *Merriam-Webster*'s links naught ("nothing") with nought as a spelling variant and a brief inclusion of naught's obsolete "evil" definition. But it makes more sense when we think of words like *naughty* and *naughtiness* that naught belongs with them. Naughty gives off juvenile vibes, true, but its original meaning was fully grown-up wickedness.

> *The righteousness of the upright shall deliver them: but transgressors shall be taken in their own naughtiness. (Proverbs 11:6)*

Everything the world pushes as worthy and important is naught (bad, evil) and will become a thing of nought (H8414), the blackest void of desolation because it is devoid of the light of Christ. The worldly will never understand your faith in Him. Never understand the concept of giving up self to the will of God. In fact, they will hate you for it. Our enemies are, in fact, enemies of God. The faithless and wicked governments of the world will unite at the end times and attempt to crush Christ and those who follow Him. They will "Take counsel together, and it shall come to nought; speak the word, and it shall not stand: for God is with us" (Isaiah 8:10). God will crush

Satan's plan and bring it to nought (H6331 to *crush, break, utterly take*), and anyone who lived by wickedness will come to their end (H657). They will be unsearchable, as if they had never existed, a thing of nought (H369).

> *They that hate thee shall be clothed with shame; and the dwelling place of the wicked shall come to nought. (Job 8:22)*

> *The Lord bringeth the counsel of the heathen to nought: he maketh the devices of the people of none effect. (Psalm 33:10)*

> *Thou shalt seek them, and shalt not find them, even them that contended with thee: they that war against thee shall be as nothing, and as a thing of nought. (Isaiah 41:12)*

We are surrounded by people who reject truth for lies and espouse false ideologies that make them feel good and bolster their delusions. Because of this, we live in a cancel culture of intimidation and societal persecution that makes a man or a woman "an offender for a word, and lay a snare for him that reproveth in the gate, and turn aside the just for a thing of nought" (Isaiah 29:21). You speak the truth and backlash will come.

The elite cabal who perpetuate this confusion, this good for nothing thing of nought (H434; H8414), who control the mainstream media, the government, the medical, scientific, and educational institutions, have and

will continue to gaslight you because they hate the truth
and think they are better and smarter than you.

> But God hath chosen the foolish things of the world
> to confound the wise; and God hath chosen the weak
> things of the world to confound the things which are
> mighty;
> And base things of the world, and things which are
> despised, hath God chosen, yea, and things which
> are not, to bring to nought things that are.
> (1 Corinthians 1:27–28)

God gives us true elite status. The wisdom and might
and the high standing the world believes they have will be
rendered entirely useless, of no effect at all when Christ
returns. Their desire to be their own god—a desert wasteland
of vanity—the same desire that corrupted Lucifer, will bring
them to nought (H656 to *disappear, cease, fail*).

> For the terrible one is brought to nought, and the
> scorner is consumed, and all that watch for iniquity
> are cut off. (Proverbs 29:20)

> For thus saith the Lord, Ye have sold yourselves for
> nought; and ye shall be redeemed without money.
> (Isaiah 52:3)

God understands our susceptibility to Satan's pull, the
many avenues we search for meaning and fulfillment, our
ragged pursuit of love and security through any means

other than Him. God knows what this has cost our souls and offers every contrite heart an invoice of redemption, a bill paid in full. He loves us that much.

[10]

Perfect

*Be ye therefore **perfect**, even as your Father which is in heaven is perfect. (Matthew 5:48)*

When you read this verse in Matthew, doesn't it make you feel inadequate? *Perfect? I'm trying, Lord, really, I am.* How are we supposed to attain this impossible standard? And why is God asking this of us when He knows are frames (Psalm 103:14)? The similar command "Be ye holy; for I am holy" found in 1 Peter 1:16 can also cause distress because we know ourselves too well. We know how far from perfect and holy we are.

Not only do we struggle in our spirits with these seemingly impossible mandates, but we're also confronted with our physical inadequacies whenever we look in the mirror or watch TV, scroll Instagram, or view air-brushed models in a magazine. A perfectionist mindset is a common proclivity for women. We want our creative skills, our writing, our art, our music, whatever skills we invest in, to

Perfect

H8549 *tāmîm*; *entire* (literally, figuratively, or morally); also (as a noun) *integrity*, *truth*:— without blemish, complete, full, sincerely, sound, undefiled, upright, whole

H8003 *šālēm* from H7999; *complete* (literally or figuratively); especially *friendly*:— full, just, made ready, peaceable, whole

H4357 *miklâ*; *completion* (in plural concretely adverbially) *wholly*:— perfect

H1585 *gĕmar* (Aramaic):— perfect

H1584 *gāmar*; to *end* (in the sense of *completion* or *failure*):— cease, come to an end, fail, perform

H8535 *tām* from H8552; *complete*; usually (morally) *pious*; specifically *gentle*, *dear*:— coupled together, plain, undefiled, upright

H8552 *tāmam*; to *complete*, in a good or bad sense:— accomplish, cease, be clean passed, consume, have done, come to an end, come to the full, be all gone, be all here, shew thyself upright, whole

H8537 *tōm* from H8552; *completeness*; figuratively *prosperity*; usually (morally) *innocent*:— fully, integrity, simplicity, uprightness

H7965 *šālôm* from H7999; *safe*, i.e. (figuratively) *well*, *happy*, *friendly*; also (abstractly) *welfare*, i.e. health, prosperity, peace:— favour, perfect peace, rest, safety, all is well

H7999 *šālam*; to *be safe* (in mind, body, estate); figuratively to *be* (*make*) *completed*, by implication to *be friendly*, by extension to *reciprocate*:— make amends, make good, pay again, make peace, restore, reward

H3632 *kālîl* from H3634; *complete*; as a noun, the *whole*, (specifically a sacrifice *entirely consumed*) as adverb fully:— all, every whit, flame, utterly, whole burnt sacrifice

H3634 *kālal*; to *complete*:— perfect, make perfect

G5046 *teleios*; *complete* (in various applications of labour, growth, mental and moral character); *completeness*:— of full age, man

G2675 *katartizō*; to *complete thoroughly*, i.e. *repair* (literally or figuratively) or *adjust*:— fit, mend, (make) perfect, perfectly join together, repair, restore

G5048 *teleioō* from G5046; to *complete*, i.e. (literally) *accomplish*, or (figuratively) *consummate* (in character):— consecrate, finish, fulfill, (make) perfect

G739 *artios*; *fresh*, i.e. (by implication) *complete*:— perfect

be perfect. We want our homes, social events we host, and businesses we run to be perfect, that glossy magazine quality of face, body, talent, and charm the world barrages us with. This desire for perfection causes immense stress and brittle emotions that snap when the inevitable failures happen.

Lucifer was created perfect in form and function, magnificently beautiful and talented. (Ezekiel 28:12–13, 15). But he turned his God-given glory into self-worship. The world follows suit by deifying physical beauty in youth, talent in performers, and wealth in billionaire entrepreneurs. The world touts plastic surgery and fat bank accounts as the fix for all that's wrong in their lives. They force divorce, abortion, and eugenics, severing anything that might complicate their perfect, godless world. But the glittering and intoxicating pride of life that caused Satan to fall and the world along with him, will never be perfect because it refuses to pursue what makes God perfect.

> *He is the Rock, his work is perfect: for all his ways are judgment: a God of truth and without iniquity, just and right is he. (Deuteronomy 32:4)*

We are told to be perfect in the KJV, but this doesn't mean being morally flawless—that's an impossibility as long as we're mortal. No, *perfect* means to be "complete" and "entire." Entirely all in. Not waffling in our faith, not wavering in our trust. Grown up and of full age, not freeze-framed babes in Christ unwilling to mature, desiring to stay young forever.

> *Howbeit we speak wisdom among them that are perfect: yet not the wisdom of this world, nor of the princes of this world, that come to nought.*
> *(1 Corinthians 2:6)*

> *For every one that useth milk is unskilful in the word of righteousness: for he is a babe.*
> *But strong meat belongeth to them that are of full age, even those who by reason of use have their senses exercised to discern both good and evil.*
> *(Hebrews 5:13–14)*

"Them that are perfect" (G5046) and "them that are of full age" (G5046) mean the same thing. As Christian women, to be of full age and perfect is to be mature in Christ, reading and studying the Word of God so our minds can wisely discern right from wrong. The Scripture was given so "that the man [and woman] of God may be perfect, throughly furnished unto all good works" (2 Timothy 3:17).

But our good works, our righteousness, our piety never stems from within us. We can never prove to God we are good apart from Him. "Is it any pleasure to the Almighty, that thou art righteous? or is it gain to him, that thou makest thy ways perfect? (Job 22:3). No. Job made this clear: "If I justify myself, mine own mouth shall condemn me: if I say, I am perfect, it shall also prove me perverse" (Job 9:20). God asks us to be "perfect" sons and daughters showing ourselves upright in how we live, but not through perfect righteousness like His. Instead, we become perfect through our complete reliance on Him. We are perfect or complete only in Christ. "And ye are complete in him, which is the head of all principality and power" (Colossians 2:10). It is a state of surrender. Not a futile effort to be like God.

Paul used the G2675 definition of perfect, meaning to *repair*, *restore*, and to *perfectly join together* when he told us to "Be perfect, be of good comfort, be of one mind, live in peace; and the God of love and peace shall be with you" (2 Corinthians 13:11). God takes our imperfect, broken parts and fits them together with divine glue for His purposes.

Now the God of peace, that brought again from the
dead our Lord Jesus, that great shepherd of the sheep,
through the blood of the everlasting covenant,
Make you perfect in every good work to do his will,
working in you that which is wellpleasing in his
sight, through Jesus Christ; to whom be glory for ever
and ever. Amen. (Hebrews 13:20–21)

God makes us perfect (G2675) by readjusting and repairing us, molding and mending us to fit perfectly together with Him. Without the indwelling Spirit of God, we cannot be complete and entire, as the Law before Christ's sacrifice proved.

For the law having a shadow of good things to come,
and not the very image of the things, can never with
those sacrifices which they offered year by year
continually make the comers thereunto perfect.
(Hebrews 10:1)

In Genesis chapter 6, we read that Noah was perfect in all his generations (Genesis 6:9). What is meant by this? Before God destroyed the earth with a flood, the generations of man were corrupted not only by incessant wickedness, but also by the communion between fallen angels and the daughters of men (Genesis 6:2–5). Noah was a man of integrity, yes, but his DNA was also physically perfect (H8549) or *uncorrupted* and *undefiled*. Those who pursue life spiritually undefiled (H8549, same definition as *perfect*) are indeed blessed (Psalm 119:1).

Thou shalt be perfect [H8549] *with the Lord thy God. (Deuteronomy 18:13)*

Let your heart therefore be perfect [H8003] *with the Lord our God, to walk in his statutes, and to keep his commandments, as at this day. (1 Kings 8:61)*

To "be perfect" with the Lord in the verses above means to be *undefiled, sincere, truthful, made ready,* and *peaceable* toward Him, willing to step up and live in obedience to His calling. This kind of perfection is only possible when we allow God's Spirit to change ours. It is God who makes us perfect; it is God who completes us. "It is God that girdeth me with strength, and maketh my way perfect" (Psalm 18:32).

The Lord will perfect that which concerneth me: thy mercy, O Lord, endureth for ever: forsake not the works of thine own hands. (Psalm 138:8)

With great confidence, we can trust everything that concerns us. Our longings, our plans, our hopes for ourselves and our families God will perfect (H1584, verb) or *perform* and *bring to an end perfectly* according to His plan. Nothing will be left to chance.

Till we all come in the unity of the faith, and of the knowledge of the Son of God, unto a perfect man, unto the measure of the stature of the fulness of Christ. (Ephesians 4:13)

The apostle Paul's wholehearted desire was to see the brethren he loved and faithfully taught enter the coming kingdom complete in Christ (Colossians 1:28). Pastors and god-fearing husbands alike have the same desire. These men are held accountable to the souls God gives them. There will be no happier moment for them than to know their fidelity and dedication made an eternal difference to those they loved and served.

Jesus Christ is the author and finisher of our faith (Hebrews 12:2). The word *finisher* (G5051; taken from the word *perfect*, G5048) means "one who completes." That being understood, reading Hebrews 2:10 brings much clarity to the text.

> *For it became him, for whom are all things, and by whom are all things, in bringing many sons unto glory, to make the captain of their salvation perfect through sufferings. (Hebrews 2:10)*

We know that suffering did not make Christ perfect, He was already perfect. Instead, the captain of our salvation suffered on the cross to *fulfill* and *complete* the righteous requirement of the Law, the blood sacrifice necessary to save us from a deserved death.

Psalm 37:37 tells us to take notice of the perfect man, for the "end of that man is peace." Being complete in Christ—living in the love of God and standing firm in His truth—brings us peace. The end of that man is more glorious than we can imagine. Christ spoke eloquently to the Father what the end (or more perfectly realized, *beginning*) for us would be: "I in them, and thou in me,

that they may be made perfect in one; and that the world
may know that thou hast sent me, and hast loved them,
as thou hast loved me" (John 17:23). Our perfection, our
completion, culminates in oneness with the Father and
the Son.

*But the God of all grace, who hath called us unto
his eternal glory by Christ Jesus, after that ye have
suffered a while, make you perfect, stablish, strengthen,
settle you. (1 Peter 5:10)*

While we wait for the glory of oneness, the epitome of
joy to be our final reality, we can't escape the suffering
from the evil this world creates. But God has promised to
keep us in perfect peace (H7965), an all-is-well, safe and
happy peace, when we keep our minds on Him.

*Thou wilt keep him in perfect peace, whose mind is
stayed on thee: because he trusteth in thee.
(Isaiah 26:3)*

11

Quick-Quicken

Thou, which hast shewed me great and sore troubles, shalt **quicken** *me again, and shalt bring me up again from the depths of the earth. (Psalm 71:20)*

Who shall give account to [Christ] that is ready to judge the **quick** *and the dead. (1 Peter 4:5)*

Hollywood has been known to sprinkle their screen-plays with Scripture now and then to appeal to a wider audience and appear culturally savvy. Rarely do they have a clue to the true meaning behind what they quote. *The Quick and the Dead*, a 1990s western, is one such example. Its title implies you had better be fast on the draw, or you won't last long on this earth. But this same phrase appears three times in the King James Version and has nothing to do with speed.

Quick

H4241 *miḥyâ* taken from H2421; *preservation of life*, hence *sustenance*; also the live flesh, i.e. the *quick*:— preserve life, recover selves, reviving

H2416 *hay* taken from H2421; *alive*; hence *raw* (flesh); *fresh* (plant, water, year), *strong*; *life* (or living thing):— age, alive, beast, congregation, life, lifetime, living creature

G2198 *zaō*; to *live*, (literally or figuratively):— life, lifetime, live, alive, lively

Quicken

H2421 *hāyâ*; to *live*, (literally or figuratively) to *revive*:— keep alive, leave alive, make life, promise life, let live, preserve alive, recover, restore, save alive, God save

G2227 *zōopoieō*; to *vitalize*, *revitalize* (literally or figuratively):— make alive, give life

Quickened H2421: see definition above

G2227: see definition above

G4806 *syzōopoieō*; to *reanimate conjointly* with (figuratively):— quicken together with

Quickeneth G2227: see definition above

Quickening G2227: see definition above

*And he commanded us to preach unto the people,
and to testify that it is he which was ordained of
God to be the Judge of quick and dead. (Acts 10:42)*

*I charge thee therefore before God, and the Lord
Jesus Christ, who shall judge the quick and the dead
at his appearing and his kingdom. (2 Timothy 4:1)*

None of the instances of the word *quick* found in the KJV Bible refers to being fast, speedy, hasty, or swift. Not one. Quick in the above scriptural references means *alive*. Whoa, what? Yes, quick (*zaō*, G2198) means "to live." As a trivial aside, the phrase *cut to the quick*, in literal or figurative context, referring to the live and painful flesh sure makes more sense now, doesn't it? But Peter in the book of Acts and Timothy in 2 Timothy were talking about God's judgment of those who had died and those who would still be alive at Christ's return as well as those who would be resurrected after the thousand-year span of His kingdom (see Revelation chapter 20).

There are two resurrections mentioned in Scripture. The first resurrection takes place at Christ's second coming immediately following the great tribulation and the binding of Satan to the bottomless pit (Matthew 24:29–31; Revelation 20:3). Those who have died *in Christ* since creation will rise first (1 Thessalonians 4:15–17), and every believer still standing will be changed into a spirit being in the twinkling of an eye (now that's quick!) and reign with Christ a thousand years (Daniel 7:27; 2 Timothy 2:12; Revelation 5:10; 20:5).

Every soul *not called by God* who died prior to Christ's millennial kingdom will be resurrected in the second resurrection. They will be taught God's righteous ways by us godly beings who will teach and govern them under Christ's rule. But they will also be influenced by Satan because when the second resurrection occurs at the end of the millennium, the enemy will be loosed from his chains and deceive the nations again (Revelation 20:3, 7–8)! The second resurrection crescendos to the great white throne judgment where those who lived and made their choice for or against Christ during the millennium or who were resurrected and did the same after will be judged out of the Book of Life (Revelation 20:11–12). Regardless of the timeline—before, during, or after the millennium—God will judge the quick and the dead.

> *If it had not been the Lord who was on our side,*
> *when men rose up against us:*
> *Then they had swallowed us up quick, when their*
> *wrath was kindled against us. (Psalm 124:2–3)*

The psalmist rightly said that if God were not by our side, our enemies would have swallowed us alive. (Isn't that the truth!) In Numbers 16:30, God opened the earth to swallow up the rebellion of Korah, Dathan, and Abiram. "They [will] go down quick into the pit." Yes, once again quick is not referring to speed or swiftness in the judgment, although invariably it was swift, but that the ground swallowed them alive. And ten times in Psalm 119, the psalmist cried out to God to quicken him (H2421 *promise life, revive, save alive)* according to God's Word, His righteousness, judgments, and loving-kindness

> *For the word of God is quick, and powerful, and sharper than any twoedged sword, piercing even to the dividing asunder of soul and spirit, and of the joints and marrow, and is a discerner of the thoughts and intents of the heart. (Hebrews 4:12)*

The Word of God is alive. It is filled with life-giving truth and fearful judgment. We have everything we need for life and godliness resting within the pages of God's book. The Word of God attests to the Word of life, Jesus Christ:

> *Who being the brightness of his glory, and the express image of his person, and upholding all things by the word of his power, when he had by himself purged our sins, sat down on the right hand of the Majesty of high. (Hebrews 1:3)*

Christ, the Bread of life, the Manna from heaven, spoke to His disciples about physical and spiritual sustenance saying, "It is the spirit that quickeneth; the flesh profiteth nothing: the words that I speak unto you, they are spirit, and they are life" (John 6:63).

> *But if the Spirit of him that raised up Jesus from the dead dwell in you, he that raised up Christ from the dead shall also quicken your mortal bodies by his Spirit that dwelleth in you. (Romans 8:11)*

It is God the Father who raised up our Lord. It is God's very essence, His Spirit, that flows from the heavens and dwells inside each one of His chosen. It is through our faith in and obedience to Christ that God has promised to quicken us, to rescue us from death and revitalize us with the Spirit of His dear Son (G2227 Greek *zōopoieō*: *zōos*=alive, *poieō*= make).

> *For as the Father raiseth up the dead, and quickeneth*
> *them; even so the Son quickeneth whom he will.*
> *For the Father judgeth no man, but hath committed*
> *all judgment unto the Son. . . .*
> *Marvel not at this: for the hour is coming, in the*
> *which all that are in the graves shall hear his voice,*
> *And shall come forth; they that have done good, unto*
> *the resurrection of life; and they that have done evil,*
> *unto the resurrection of damnation.*
> *(John 5:21–22, 28–29)*

Our carnal nature condemns us to separation from a holy God. But the magnificent gift that is the Spirit of Christ within us sets us apart from the world, frees us from condemnation, and gives us strength to overcome our sins and live by the fruits of that same Spirit in love, joy, peace, patience, gentleness, goodness, faith, meekness, and self-control (Galatians 5:22–23).

> *But ye are not in the flesh, but in the Spirit, if so be*
> *that the Spirit of God dwell in you. Now if any*
> *man have not the Spirit of Christ, he is none of his.*
> *(Romans 8:9)*

We are complete in Christ,

In whom also ye are circumcised with the circumcision made without hands, in putting off the body of the sins of the flesh by the circumcision of Christ. . . .
And you being dead in your sins and the uncircumcision of your flesh, hath he quickened together with him, having forgiven you all trespasses. (Colossians 2:11, 13)

Our faith in Christ, the indwelling of His Spirit, and our daily dying to self ensure our quickening will result in a copiously rich, ever-living life at the last trump. Does not this truth abundantly comfort your soul?

For the Lord himself shall descend from heaven with a shout, with the voice of the archangel, and with the trump of God: and the dead in Christ shall rise first: Then we which are alive and remain shall be caught up together with them in the clouds, to meet the Lord in the air: and so shall we ever be with the Lord.
Wherefore comfort one another with these words. (1 Thessalonians 4:16–18)

12

Quit

*Watch ye, stand fast in the faith, **quit** you like men, be strong. (1 Corinthians 16:13)*

For those devoted to reading the King James Version Bible, nothing quite compares to the majesty, poetic beauty, and accurate rendering of the original manuscripts as the KJV does. But some passages give us pause and 1 Corinthians 16:13 is indeed one of them. Our first impulse is to think: *Quit? Real men don't quit!* How is a man supposed to watch, stand fast, be strong, and quit at the same time?

According to *Vine's Complete Expository Dictionary*, the word *quit* in 1 Corinthians 16:13 comes from the Greek word *andrizō* meaning to "play the man," or as *Strong's Concordance* puts it: to "act manly."

Watch, stand fast, act like a man ought to act, be strong. Whew! What a difference a little word study makes, hmm? In 1 Samuel 4:9, we find a similar decree issued to the Philistine army:

Quit

H5352 *nāqâ*; to *be* (or *make*) *clean* (literally or figuratively); to *be bare*, i.e. *extirpated*:— acquit at all, be blameless, clear, cleanse, be free, be guiltless, be innocent

H5355 *nāqî* from H5352; *innocent*:— blameless, clean, clear, exempted, free, guiltless, innocent

H1961 *hāyâ*; to *exist*, i.e. *be* or *become, come to pass*:— beacon, be committed, be accomplished, be like, cause, follow, happen, pertain

G407 *andrizomai*; to *act manly*:— quit

From *Merriam-Webster's Collegiate Dictionary*:

extirpate: to root out, completely destroy

Be strong, and quit yourselves like men, O ye Philistines, that ye be not servants unto the Hebrews, as they have been to you: quit yourselves like men, and fight. (1 Samuel 4:9)

Become men, be committed to being men, conduct yourselves like men. This was the call to the fearful Philistine army when they learned that the ark of the Lord was in the midst of the Israelite camp. "And the Philistines were afraid, for they said, God is come into the camp. Woe be unto us!" (1 Samuel 4:7). Funny how they wanted to fight the Israelites, but not the God of Israel. They knew of the mighty works of their enemy's God and had assuredly heard of the plagues of Egypt. No wonder they wanted to turn and run. Their hearts were melting at the very thought.

And if men strive together, and one smite another with a stone, or with his fist, and he die not, but keepeth his bed:
If he rise again, and walk abroad with his staff, then shall he that smote him be quit: only he shall pay for the loss of his time, and shall cause him to be thoroughly healed. (Exodus 21:18–19)

In the example above, the word *quit* (H5352) comes from the Hebrew word *nāqâ* and is akin to the English word *acquit*: to clear a person of a charge by declaring him not guilty; to exonerate. A similar meaning of the word *quit* (H5355) is found in Exodus:

> *If an ox gore a man or a woman, that they die: then*
> *the ox shall be surely stoned, and his flesh shall not*
> *be eaten; but the owner of the ox shall be quit.*
> *(Exodus 21:28)*

Accidents happen. But when there is no negligence or ill intent on the individual's part, God declared them quit: free of blame, exempt, and guiltless in the matter.

The book of Joshua details the story of the harlot Rahab and the Israelite spies in Jericho. Rahab knew of the mighty God of Israel, and at some point in her life, came to fear Him. She chose to align herself with God and His chosen people by risking her life in hiding these men and made a pact with the spies to save her family. The men agreed and said:

> *Behold, when we come into the land, thou shalt bind*
> *this scarlet thread in the window which thou didst*
> *let us down by: and thou shalt bring thy father, and*
> *thy mother, and thy brethren, and all thy father's*
> *household, home unto thee.*
> *And it shall be, that whosoever shall go out of the*
> *doors of thy house into the street, his blood shall be*
> *upon his head, and we will be guiltless: and*
> *whosoever shall be with thee in the house, his blood*
> *shall be on our head, if any hand be upon him.*
> *And if thou utter this our business, then we will be*
> *quit of thine oath which thou hast made us to swear.*
> *And she said, According to your words, so be it.*
> *(Joshua 2:18–21)*

Whether between men and women in business, a man and wife in marriage, or between mankind and God, swearing an oath was binding with serious repercussions if not honored. Therefore, the spies stipulated that their oath would become void if Rahab did not keep her word. They essentially said, "If you don't hold up your end of the bargain, then we're clear of our promise to you. We won't be held accountable."

But Rahab was true to her word and embarked on a new path of faith and obedience to God. She could have been forgotten in the annals of history, but God made it a point to teach us, through her example, that no matter where we start, if we repent and turn away from our sins, we will be quit (made clean, be guiltless, blameless) before Him.

By faith the harlot Rahab perished not with them that believed not, when she had received the spies with peace. (Hebrews 11:31)

The word *quit* is only used five times in the King James Version, but for the sake of thoroughness, it should be mention that the word does appear once in Luke 12:58 of the American Standard Version (1901). "For as thou art going with thine adversary before the magistrate, on the way give diligence to be quit of him; lest haply he drag thee unto the judge, and the judge shall deliver thee to the officer, and the officer shall cast thee into prison." The ASV's use of the phrase "to be quit" comes from the Greek word *apallassō*, meaning to be freed from or released, as from a lawsuit.

The same verse in the KJV uses the phrase "be delivered" (G525) instead.

Throughout the Bible, God requires both His sons and His daughters to

- ❀ Watch: be aware of what's going on in the world so we're not deceived, and be aware of the devil's schemes so we're not caught unawares and tempted.
- ❀ Stand fast: be fixed in a stable position where we don't wobble or vacillate in our faith, but persevere.
- ❀ Be strong: be entirely reliant on the power of God (Matthew 26:41; Philippians 4:1; Ephesians 6:10).

But what if 1 Corinthians 16:13 were specifically addressed to us women? How would we "quit you like women"?

Watch ye, stand fast in the faith, quit you like [women], be strong. (1 Corinthians 16:13, emphasis added)

We've all heard the phrase "man up" and when a man is told this (whether the speaker realizes it or not), he's expected to gather in himself all the good things that make him a man: his decisiveness, his strength, his bravery, his protectiveness, his self-sacrifice, and live it, not back down or turn back, and brandish these God-given masculine traits to tackle his circumstances because God put those traits in him for the man's glory and for His own.

When we act like women by our tenderness, fortitude, loyalty, willingness, encouragement, empathy, industriousness, discretion, and quiet spirit, equal glory is bestowed to God and given to us. Our womanliness, our femininity, is a gilded treasure we reflect. It's what makes us pleasing in the sight of God and man.

Now that we know "quit you like men" means to act manly or play the man (as if standing on a stage built by God and handed a divine script), let us women apply this verse to ourselves, giving God the glory His name deserves as we act like the holy women the Author of life created us to be.

[13]

Recompence/Recompense

*Yea, and what have ye to do with me, O Tyre, and Zidon, and all the coasts of Palestine? will ye render me a **recompence**? and if ye **recompense** me, swiftly and speedily will I return your recompence upon your own head. (Joel 3:4)*

In the King James Version, we will find the English word *recompense* spelled two ways: recompence and recompense. Both are used throughout the Bible, and it might seem arbitrary which spelling is used when. The key to this conundrum is knowing that one spelling is used for the noun form and the other for the verb form. Like the words *prophecy* and *prophesy*, and *council* and *counsel*, the "c" denotes the noun, the thing itself, and the "s" denotes the verb, the action being done.

The main definition of recompence is "requital." Both words, *recompence* and *requital*, are fancy ways of saying a return for something done, whether good or bad. Payback,

Recompence

H8005 *šillēm* from H7999; *requital:*— recompence

H8545 *tĕmûrâ*; *barter, compensation:*— change, exchange, restitution

H1576 *gĕmûl* from H1580; *treatment*; i.e. an *act* (of good or ill); by implication *service* or *requital:*— benefit, deserving, reward

H7966 *šillûm* from H7999; a *requital*, i.e. (secure) *retribution*, a *fee:*— reward

G468 *antapodoma* from G467; a *requital* (properly the thing):— recompence

G489 *antimisthia*; *requital, correspondence:*— recompence

G3405 *misthapodosia*; *requital* (good or bad):— recompence of reward

Recompences H7966: see above

H1578 *gĕmûlâ* feminine of H1576; meaning the same:— deed, recompense, such a reward

Recompense

H7725 *šûb*; *turn back*, literally or figuratively; generally to *retreat*; *again:*— do anything again, recover, relieve, rescue, render again, restore, turn self again, turn from

H7999 *šālam*; to *be safe* (in mind, body, estate); figuratively to *be* (*make*) *completed*, by implication to *be friendly*, by extension to *reciprocate:*— make amends, make good, pay again, make peace, restore, reward

H1580 *gāmal*; to *treat a person* (well or ill), i.e. *benefit* or *require*; by implication (of *toil*) to *ripen*, i.e. (specifically) to *wean*:— deal bountifully, do good, reward, serve, yield

H5414 *nātan*; to *give*, used with great latitude of application (*put, make*, etc.):— add, assign, avenge, be healed, bestow, deliver, distribute, grant, lay unto charge, ordain, pay, perform, render, trade, willingly, would God

G467 *antapodidomi* from G591; to *requite* (good or evil):— render, repay

G591 *apodidōmi*; to *give away*, i.e. *up, over, back*:— deliver (again), give (again), pay, repay, perform, render, requite, restore, reward, sell, yield

Recompensed H7725: see above

H7999: see above, same for Recompensest

H5414: see above, also same for Recompensing

G467: see above

comeuppance, a friendly exchange, or a reward. According to *Merriam-Webster's,* requital means *something given in return, compensation,* or *retaliation.*

God is the God of "recompences" (Jeremiah 51:56). He alone is the righteous judge. He will mete out reward or punishment to all of mankind at the appointed time. God says,

> *To me belongeth vengeance, and recompence; their foot shall slide in due time: for the day of their calamity is at hand, and the things that shall come upon them make haste. (Deuteronomy 32:35)*

The governments of this world have persecuted and stifled the freedoms of its citizens for their own gain for millennia. And the elite of our day are no different. They repeatedly lie and put up smokescreens to hide behind while they thwart the truth without retribution. They are convinced no one can touch them, and they get away with their deeds because they breed fear through their power. But we have recourse. We can pray as Jeremiah did. "Render unto them a recompence, O Lord, according to the work of their hands" (Lamentations 3:64). And God will.

Say to them that are of a fearful heart, Be strong, fear not: behold, your God will come with vengeance, even God with a recompence; he will come and save you. (Isaiah 35:4)

Now is the end come upon thee, and I will send mine anger upon thee, and will judge thee according to thy ways, and will recompense upon thee all thine abominations. (Ezekiel 7:3)

Injustices abound in this godless society. It grieves our spirits and we want to make it right. There are times when we can make it right with God's blessing. But other times, we need to step back and remember God has already promise to make everything right in His millennial kingdom. "Say not thou, I will recompense evil; but wait on the Lord, and he shall save thee" (Proverbs 20:22). He will save us from the evil perpetrated upon us from wicked men and women, but most importantly, He will save us from our own sinfulness. But what if we are treated badly by a husband, a family member, or a friend? People that we love? When we are wronged, the adversarial spirit insists we repay them (G591) in the same heartless manner, to "make them pay" for the pain and unkindness they inflicted upon us we did not deserve. Our carnal desire for revenge, our tit for tat, is strong, but God is stronger. When we are tethered to God's indwelling Spirit, the fruits of self-control and long-suffering are a recompense He provides to combat the enemy, so we can forgive and get off the nauseating circuit of the evil-for-evil merry-go-round Satan constructed.

Recompense to no man evil for evil. Provide things honest in the sight of all men. (Romans 12:17)

Not rendering evil for evil, or railing for railing: but contrariwise blessing; knowing that ye are thereunto called, that ye should inherit a blessing. (1 Peter 3:9)

Whether young or old, we often hold a false idea that we deserve better than what we've been given. With this mindset, we fail to be humble, become angry more easily, and compare our lot with others. We put our hopes in the vanity of life, but what do we get in return? The dissatisfaction of ever-changing physical things incapable of providing contentment. "Let not him that is deceived trust in vanity: for vanity shall be his recompence" (Job 15:31). God knows what we need. He will not coddle us by giving us our every whim when those whims only keep us spiritually stagnant and replace our reliance on Him with the fickle satisfaction of trinkets. God wants strong, faithful women who know that without Him and the covering afforded by Jesus Christ, we deserve nothing but death.

"Behold, the righteous shall be recompensed in the earth: much more the wicked and the sinner" (Proverbs 11:31). The beauty of the mercy of God is He won't recompense the evil in us as we deserve. God looks upon us draped in the mantle of His Son; we can rest in His compassion. Our identity as Christian women is rooted in the righteousness of Christ, and we will be recompensed, an undeserved but glorious exchange, with eternal life nothing else can compare to.

> *Esteeming the reproach of Christ greater riches than the treasures in Egypt: for he had respect unto the recompence of the reward. (Hebrews 11:26)*

Moses "had it all" from a worldly standpoint. Fame, riches, a highly coveted position. But he traded it all for what those around him would call a fool's barter—kinship with Christ. Moses and others throughout biblical history understood the difference between what could be wrested from a physical life and waiting for and respecting the Rewarder of spiritual life.

> *But without faith it is impossible to please him: for he that cometh to God must believe that he is, and that he is a rewarder of them that diligently seek him. (Hebrews 11:6)*

Like Moses, we have chosen to do the same. Instead of pursuing what gives us temporary pleasures, we know there is a recompense of reward. A reward promised that is worth the suffering, the ridicule, the earthly insecurities for the security of eternity with God. "Cast not away therefore your confidence, which hath great recompence of reward" (Hebrews 10:35). Our faith in God might never draw blood as it does in other countries, but then again, as we get closer to the end times, it might. Yet whether we live or die, our work of faith—obedience to the Word of God, loving our fellow man, and overcoming our desires to rule ourselves—will not be forgotten.

The Lord recompense thy work, and a full reward be given thee of the Lord God of Israel, under whose wings thou art come to trust. (Ruth 2:12)

Everything you've struggled with, all the pain you've had to live through, will have meaning. None of it will be lost or wasted. Because you trust God and are willing to sit still at His throne, God will deal bountifully with you. An impossible recompense you can never repay.

And thou shalt be blessed; for they cannot recompense thee: for thou shalt be recompensed at the resurrection of the just. (Luke 14:14)

Repent

Therefore I will judge you, O house of Israel, every one according to his ways, saith the Lord God. **Repent,** *and turn yourselves from all your transgressions; so iniquity shall not be your ruin. (Ezekiel 18:30)*

The word *repent* is pretty straightforward. Open any dictionary, and you'll find it means "to feel regret or sorrow for past sins" with an "attempt to make amends." But if this definition was all there was to it, then why does the KJV Bible say God repents? There must be more to this word's ancient meaning than we think. And there is.

And it repented the Lord that he had made man on the earth, and it grieved him at his heart. (Genesis 6:6)

For the Lord will judge his people, and he will repent himself concerning his servants. (Psalm 135:14)

Repent

H5162 *nāham*; properly to *sigh*, i.e. *breathe* strongly; by implication to *be sorry*, i.e. (in a favorable sense) to *pity*, *console* or *rue* [see definition below]; or (unfavorably) to *avenge* (oneself):— comfort, ease oneself

H7725 *šûb*; *turn back*, literally or figuratively; generally to *retreat*; *again*:— do anything again, recover, relieve, rescue, render again, restore, turn self again, turn from

G3340 *metanoeō*; to *think differently* or *afterwards*, i.e. *reconsider* (morally *feel compunction*):— repent

G3338 *metamelomai*; to *care afterwards*, i.e. *regret*:— repent (self)

Repentance H5164 *nōḥam* from H5162; *ruefulness*, i.e. desistance [see defintion below]:— repentance

G3341 *metanoia* from G3340; *compunction* [see definition below] (for guilt, including *reformation*); by implication *reversal* (of [another's] decision):— repentance

G278 *ametamelētos*; *irrevocable*:— not to be repented of

Repented H5162: see definition above

G3340: see definition above

G3338: see definition above

G278: see above

Repentest H5162: see definition above

Repenteth H5162 and **G3340**: see definitions above

Repenting H5150 *nīḥûm* from H5162; properly *consoled*; abstractly *solace*:— comfort, comfortable

From *Merriam-Webster's Collegiate Dictionary*:
compunction: *1a*: anxiety arising from awareness of guilt; *1b*: distress of mind over an anticipated action or result; *2*: a twinge of misgiving: scruple
desistance: to cease to proceed or act, stop
rue: *n.* regret, sorrow, *vb.* to feel penitence, remorse, or regret

Thou hast forsaken me, saith the Lord, thou art gone backward: therefore will I stretch out my hand against thee, and destroy thee; I am weary with repenting. (Jeremiah 15:6)

In these three verses, repent and repented (H5162) mean to "sigh," a deep "breath of consolation or regret" to ease oneself. In Genesis, Psalms, and Jeremiah above, God is sorry for the results of His children's actions, but has consoled Himself in His righteous judgment.

And it came to pass, when Pharaoh had let the people go, that God led them not through the way of the land of the Philistines, although that was near; for God said, Lest peradventure the people repent when they see war, and they return to Egypt. (Exodus 13:17)

In Exodus 13:17, it is the Israelites whom God did not want to sigh regretfully, a downcast exhale, because of the choice they made to flee Egypt. He did not want them to be sorry for following Him and to go back to servitude because of their fear of the unknown.

God repents one other way: He changes His mind. "Who can tell if God will turn and repent, and turn away from his fierce anger, that we perish not?" (Jonah 3:9). But look at what the KJV says God changes His mind from doing? "And the Lord repented of the evil which he thought to do unto his people" (Exodus 32:14). *Of the evil?* What do we make of this?

> *And when the angel stretched out his hand upon Jerusalem to destroy it, the Lord repented him of the evil, and said to the angel that destroyed the people, It is enough: stay now thine hand.* (2 Samuel 24:16)

> *Therefore now amend your ways and your doings, and obey the voice of the Lord your God; and the Lord will repent him of the evil that he hath pronounced against you.* (Jeremiah 26:13)

The KJV translators struggled in translating some Hebrew and Greek words into English, and the word *evil* was one of them. We all know that evil is the opposite of who God is, therefore God cannot do anything evil. He is not the author of evil. Satan is. When the Bible uses the word *evil* in relation to God's actions, it means He causes affliction, calamity, and adversity to rightly affect people's lives. "Repented him of the evil" means God changed His mind from dispensing affliction on those who deserved it.

But the KJV also tells us God will *not* repent in certain situations. He does not go back and forth with uncertainty or change His mind on a whim as mankind does. He cannot be sorry for His righteous decisions.

> *God is not a man, that he should lie; neither the son of man, that he should repent: hath he said, and shall he not do it? or hath he spoken, and shall he not make it good? (Numbers 23:19)*

> *The Lord hath sworn, and will not repent, Thou art a priest for ever after the order of Melchizedek. (Psalm 110:4)*

> *I the Lord have spoken it: it shall come to pass, and I will do it; I will not go back, neither will I spare, neither will I repent; according to thy ways, and according to thy doings, shall they judge thee, saith the Lord God. (Ezekiel 24:14)*

Now that we've learned how God does and does not repent, what does it mean for us to repent? Digging into the multifaceted definition, repent means to *reconsider* our courses of action, to *think differently* than what comes naturally to us (G3340), to *turn back* to God (H7725), and with our God-given sense of remorse and guilt (H5162; G3341), *reverse* the selfish way we live, and *go back home* to Him (H7725). "I thought on my ways, and turned my feet unto thy testimonies" (Psalm 119:59).

Repent ye therefore, and be converted, that your sins
may be blotted out, when the times of refreshing
shall come from the presence of the Lord. (Acts 3:19)

We come to Christ through the Father's calling, realize
how much we need His mercy and saving power in our
lives, and begin the process of changing how we live to
show our love and gratitude. We could never be converted
if we didn't initially repent first, didn't turn around and
face God; we receive His Holy Spirit once we do (Acts
2:38). But although conversion is a one-time event,
repentance is an on-going one until we die. Repentance is
like labor pains. We women cannot stay pregnant forever,
pregnant with the sorrows of the knowledge of our sins
without doing the painful work of pushing away the sins
themselves, to reconsider our skewed sense of justice, our
desire for autonomy, and our distrust in God we would
never admit out loud.

Or despisest thou the riches of his goodness and
forbearance and longsuffering; not knowing that
the goodness of God leadeth thee to repentance?
(Romans 2:4)

Esau sought repentance carefully with tears and yet
failed to achieve it. Why? Because although he felt the
sadness, he felt the anguish associated with guilt and
remorse for his decisions, he left it there; he didn't take
the next step. The beginning of repentance is a heavy
feeling of remorse over sins and a desire to change, yes,

but we must take that desire all the way to the end, like birth. Acknowledging our ways of thinking are indefensible and telling ourselves *no more.* To avoid an Esau impasse, ask yourself some questions. Why do I struggle with submitting to my husband, loving my neighbor as myself, forgiving those who've hurt me, and why do I worry that God won't make my life good enough unless I intervene? Do I truly believe God's ways are righteous? Then why do I balk at obedience?

> *In meekness instructing those that oppose themselves;*
> *if God peradventure will give them repentance to*
> *the acknowledging of the truth. (2 Timothy 2:25)*

Repentance is a repeated action in the life of a Christian, a deep soul-searching that finds every hidden belief, every rigid and headstrong thought, and hands it over to Christ. It may take months, years, or even decades before we can fling the treasured idols of self away. But the ability to change, the strength needed to wrench our self-interests from their stubbornly fixed position and glide the turnstile of our hearts to face God comes from God Himself.

> *For godly sorrow worketh repentance to salvation*
> *not to be repented of: but the sorrow of the world*
> *worketh death. (2 Corinthians 7:10)*

Paul spoke volumes in this one sentence. Sorrow can be good and healthy or useless and self-serving. Our feelings of sorrow birthed from the pangs of anxiety and regret, the distress of mind that conflicts with our conscience toward God are necessary to begin the work of repentance. Merely being sorry won't get us anywhere as Esau proved. True repentance is essential for salvation. Jesus Christ spoke this often in His time on earth (Matthew 4:17; 11:20; Luke 13:3, 5). Paul explained in 2 Corinthians that it is our repenting work that bears salvation, a salvation "not to be repented of" (G278). The word *repented* in this packed-full sentence means "irrevocable." Our repentance leads to salvation that cannot be altered or taken away. "For the gifts and calling of God are without repentance" (Romans 11:29). How comforting it is to know God will not turn back on His promises.

No matter what sins we turn away from: addiction, hatred, gossip, adultery from our past, or a seemingly innocuous sorry-for-ourselves scowl and a perpetual spirit of complaint, if we choose to wake with a smile and a quiet spirit instead, God and a million million angels rejoice.

Likewise, I say unto you, there is joy in the presence of the angels of God over one sinner that repenteth. (Luke 15:10)

[15]

Sober

*Be **sober**, be vigilant; because your adversary the devil, as a roaring lion, walketh about, seeking whom he may devour. (1 Peter 5:8)*

Sober is a word that automatically conjures thoughts of alcohol intake, self-restraint, and a popular twelve-step program. But surprisingly, this word in our King James Version Bibles has little to do with our glasses of wine and more to do with our states of mind.

If you look closely at the book of Titus, you will notice the word *sober* is used four times in chapters 1–2, but further research reveals that each time the word is used, it means something different. That's right. In Titus, *sober* has four separate, completely non-alcoholic meanings.

*For a bishop must be ... a lover of hospitality, a lover of good men, **sober**, just, holy, temperate. (Titus 1:7–8)*

Sober

G4993 *sōphroneō* from G4998; to *be of sound mind*, i.e. *sane*, (figuratively) *moderate*:— be in [your] right mind

G3525 *nēphō* to *abstain* from wine (*keep sober*), i.e. (figuratively) *be discreet*:— be sober, watch

G4998 *sōphrōn*; safe (sound) in *mind*, i.e. *self-controlled* (moderate as to opinion or passion):— discreet, temperate

G3524 *nēphaleos* from G3525; *sober*, i.e. (figuratively) circumspect:— sober

G4994 *sōphronizō* from G4998; to *make of sound mind*, i.e. (figuratively) to *discipline* or *correct*:— teach [or train] to be sober

Soberly G4993: see definition above

G4996 *sōphronōs* adverb from G4998; *with sound mind*, i.e. *moderately*:— soberly

Soberness G4997 *sōphrosynē* from G4998; *soundness of mind*, i.e. (literally) *sanity* or (figuratively) *self-control*:— sobriety

Sobriety G4997: see definition above

Sober Minded G4993: see definition above

From *Merriam–Webster's Collegiate Dictionary*:

circumspect: careful to consider all circumstances and consequences; prudent (cautious, discreet)

temperate: not extreme or excessive

That the aged men be **sober***, grave, temperate, sound in faith, in charity, in patience. (Titus 2:2)*

That they [the aged women] *teach the young women to be* **sober***, to love their husbands, to love their children. (Titus 2:4)*

Young men likewise exhort to be **sober** *minded. (Titus 2:6)*

Let's see how the King James translators defined the word *sober* for each verse:

1. **sound of mind:** safe, stable, self-controlled (1:8)
2. **vigilant:** staying watchful and alert to danger or trouble; and circumspect: cautious and careful before acting, judging, or deciding (2:2)
3. **wise:** having or showing good [that is, morally true] judgment, having disciplined minds (2:4)
4. **discreet:** careful about what one says or does; moderate [emotionally, neither hot nor cold] (2:6)

Word study certainly brings to light our understanding of God's Word, doesn't it? Of the four uses of sober, we find door number three chiseled with this message for older women: teach the younger women to be wise. With all the emotional baggage, the hormonal ups and downs, the crazy life circumstances, and the little ones (not to mention their dear husbands) always needing something, the stress takes its toll, and wisdom in speech and actions does not spring spontaneously for younger women under a normal load, let alone a heavy one. But with God's Spirit and the training and guidance of godly older women who've "been there, done that," they can learn to leave emotionalism at the door and cross the threshold as sober-minded women.

Our minds are the staging point for every battle we face, and we women—young and old alike—must bring "every thought captive to the obedience of Christ" (2 Corinthians 10:5). Doing so will stop the fears, the wants, the daily frustrations, as well as the flitting and fickle emotions we unwittingly house from dictating a negative and faithless response.

In 2 Timothy 1:7, the apostle Paul let us in on a most profound endowment: "For God hath not given us a spirit of fear; but of power, and of love, and of a sound mind." God has given us His power to overcome evil, His love to filter each day through. He has given us disciplined minds, so we can judge with righteous judgment (John 7:24) and not be tossed to and fro by the winds of doctrine (Ephesians 4:14). Sobriety is a state of mind. We sober-minded Christians choose to heed the many warnings in the Bible and stay alert to spiritual dangers. We watch, as faithful night guards, for we know our enemy is cunning and waits in the dark for those who willingly nod into spiritual sleep.

> *Therefore let us not sleep as do others; but let us watch and be sober.*
> *For they that sleep sleep in the night; and they that be drunken are drunken in the night.*

But let us, who are of the day, be sober, putting on
the breastplate of faith and love; and for an helmet,
the hope of salvation. (1 Thessalonians 4:6–8)

The Bible is patently clear we are not to live a lifestyle of drunkenness—because how can we be watchful of world events and stay alert to spiritual dangers if we are desensitized?—but to merely abstain from alcohol does not make one sober-minded. We might not drink a drop, yet stagger drunkenly on our emotions, driving desires, self-righteous behavior, complacency, and the seductive offerings of this age.

God gave us the fruit of the vine to enjoy (Judges 9:13; Psalm 104:15). He gave us tantalizing foods to consume and sexual pleasures within marriage too. But all these gifts can be used and abused for selfish and ungodly means. The call to live soberly is a call for righteous thinking whether we drink alcohol or not. It is a call

- ❧ To be wise virgins prepared for the return of our Bridegroom
- ❧ To say no to anyone or anything that could hinder our vigilance
- ❧ To be watchful of world affairs (from the least-biased sources we can find, a monumental feat, to be sure) so nothing deceives us and leaves us unprepared like the ten foolish virgins who were shut out of the Bridegroom's chamber (Matthew 25:5–13)

Take ye heed, watch and pray: for ye know not when
the time is. . . .
Watch ye therefore: for ye know not when the master
of the house cometh, at even, or at midnight, or at
the cockcrowing, or in the morning:
Lest coming suddenly he find you sleeping.
And what I say unto you I say unto all, Watch.
(Mark 13:33, 35–37)

As we watch and pray, we train our minds in wisdom. We take our calling seriously and conduct ourselves with godly sanity in a desperately insane world.

But the grace of God that bringeth salvation hath
appeared to all men,
Teaching us that, denying ungodliness and worldly
lusts, we should live soberly, righteously, and godly,
in this present world. (Titus 2:11–12)

Sober-mindedness is the conscious decision to acknowledge God's truth and wisdom above our own and to live level-headed and even-tempered amid the chaos of our days. When we "live soberly," we become aware of people and situations that might stifle the Spirit of God within us—the Spirit that keeps us sane.

And be not conformed to this world: but be ye
transformed by the renewing of your mind, that ye
may prove what is that good, and acceptable, and
perfect, will of God.

For I say, through the grace given unto me, to every
man that is among you, not to think of himself more
highly than he ought to think; but to think soberly,
according as God hath dealt to every man the
measure of faith. (Romans 12:2–3)

Thinking soberly is being in your right mind—a safe
and sound mind (G4998 *sōphrōn: sōzō*, to save, *phrēn*, the
mind). A mind awake to God's righteousness, one that
speaks words of truth and soberness (G4997 *sōphrosynē*,
sanity). "But the end of all things is at hand: be ye therefore
sober, and watch unto prayer" (1 Peter 4:7).

We live in sobering times, dear women. Evil masquer-
ades as angels of light in every domain of life, but never
fear—God has given us the discerning, sober mind of
Christ (1 Corinthians 2:16).

Wherefore gird up the loins of your mind, be sober,
and hope to the end for the grace that is to be brought
unto you at the revelation of Jesus Christ.
(1 Peter 1:13)

16

Strait

*Enter ye in at the **strait** gate: for wide is the gate, and broad is the way, that leadeth to destruction, and many there be which go in thereat. (Matthew 7:13)*

D o not be embarrassed if you thought the word *strait* was just a quaint, old-fashioned spelling for the word *straight* in the KJV. You wouldn't be the first. But if you think of these two words as interchangeable in your mind's eye, you'll miss the insight strait gives to several key verses. Let the words *straitjacket*, *strait-laced*, and the *Strait of Gibraltar* that grace your dictionary give you a pressed-from-all-sides clue.

Have you ever felt the cliff walls of your life hem you in, and with labored sighs of despair, tripped over loose stones and falling debris of a miscarriage, a cancer diagnosis, or out-of-reach dreams? Have you ever found yourself wedged in the unenviable position of having to choose between your family, friends, or the seemingly perfect job opportunity and Christ? If so, then you, dear woman, were in a strait.

Strait

H6887 *ṣārar*; to *cramp* (literally or figuratively):—
adversary, afflict, besiege, bind, bind up, distress,
narrower, oppress, pangs, shut up, be in trouble, vex

H6862 *ṣar* from H6887; *narrow*, a *tight* place,
(figuratively i.e. *trouble*); also a *pebble*; an *opponent* (as
crowding):— enemy, foe, affliction, close, distress,
narrow, small, sorrow, tribulation

G4728 *stenos*; *narrow* (from obstacles *standing* close
about):— strait

G4912 *synechō*; to *hold together*, i.e. to *compress* (the
ears, with a crowd or siege) or *arrest* (a prisoner);
figuratively to *compel*, *perplex*, *afflict*:— constrain,
hold, stop, keep in, throng

Straiten H6693 *ṣûq*; to *compass*, i.e. (figuratively)
oppress, *distress*:— constrain, press

Straitened H3334 *yāṣar*; to *press*, i.e. be *narrow*,
figuratively *be in distress*:— be distressed, be narrow,
be vexed

H4164 *mûṣaq*; *narrowness*; figuratively *distress*:—
anguish

H680 *āṣal*; properly to *join*; to *separate*; hence to
select, *refuse*, *contract*:— keep, reserve, take

H7114 *qāṣar*; to *dock off*, i.e. *curtail*; especially to
harvest (grass or grain):— cut down, grieve, mourn,
reap, be shorter, trouble, vex

G4912: see definition above

G4729 *stenochōreō*; to *hem* in closely, (figuratively)
cramp:— distress

Straiteneth H5148 *nāḥâ*; to *guide*; to *transport*:—
bestow, bring, govern, lead, lead forth

Straitness H4689 *māṣôq*; a *narrow* place, i.e.

(figuratively and abstractly) *confinement* or *disability*:—
anguish, distress

H4164: see definition above

Straits H3334: see definition above

H4712 *mēṣar* something *tight*, i.e. (figuratively)
trouble:— distress, pain

A strait may be straight, but not necessarily. Most often this tight passage has curves, and with certainty, it constricts as it twists, giving you very little room to move about. Our faithfulness to God puts us in a difficult spot, a narrow strait with the world around us. We know what we *have* to do, but we're stuck shoulder-to-shoulder with anger, sadness, and fear. It is this claustrophobic place that hampers our steps and creates great distress.

> *And David said unto God, I am in a great strait: let us fall into the hand of the Lord; for his mercies are great: and let me not fall into the hand of man.*
> *(2 Samuel 24:14)*

When so much in life hurts and causes you pain, when you're en route through the Strait of Affliction and see no way out, do what David did. Fall into the outstretched hands of your merciful God. And fear not; God is mighty to save! He cannot be straitened (H7114) or be *cut off*, *curtailed*, or *made shorter*. He is not hampered or constrained by a single thing.

> *O thou that are named the house of Jacob, is the*
> *spirit of the Lord straitened? are these his doings?*
> *do not my words do good to him that walketh*
> *uprightly? (Micah 2:7)*

As women of God, we walk "the straight and narrow" turning our backs on the world's perverse and crooked path, embrace the Lordship of Christ, and in so doing become set apart and beloved daughters. The straight and narrow is a strait that swaddles us with God's truth and holds us tightly in His love. It only becomes claustrophobic when we fight the confines He's created.

> *The steps of his strength shall be straitened, and his*
> *own counsel shall cast him down. (Job 18:7)*

> *In the fullness of his sufficiency he shall be in straits:*
> *every hand of the wicked shall come upon him.*
> *(Job 20:22)*

> *Judah is gone into captivity because of affliction, and*
> *because of great servitude: she dwelleth among the*
> *heathen, she findeth no rest: all her persecutors overtook*
> *her between the straits. (Lamentations 1:3)*

Throughout the Old Testament, Israel and Judah often found themselves straitened by their own doing. This set apart and beloved people chose self-reliance, haughtiness, and disobedience to God. Therefore, God used their enemies to wedge them between a rock and a hard place.

Now that we understand the meaning of the word *strait*, Christ's call for us to enter the "strait gate" recorded in Matthew and Luke makes much more sense. This gate is no ordinary, easy-to-get-through gate with oiled hinges and a gentle latch you wouldn't use anyway because the gate is so low you could leap over it. No. This gate that leads to everlasting life requires us to strive to enter through it. We must:

❀ fight the adversary daily,
❀ labor in the heat of the day fervently, and
❀ struggle with the world (and ourselves) every step of the way.

This is too much work for lackadaisical Christians to bother with. They may halfheartedly seek this narrow opening, but wish to enter in on their own terms. For all their self-centered attempts, the gate is impossible to find.

> *Enter ye in at the strait gate: for wide is the gate, and broad is the way, that leadeth to destruction, and many there be which go in thereat:*
> *Because strait is the gate, and narrow is the way, that leadeth unto life, and few there be that find it.*
> *(Matthew 7:13–14)*

The way to destruction is wide and smooth, a grassy meadow on a fair day. The stride is easy, the view serene. To traverse this path, you don't need to examine yourself or repent. You don't need to give up your desires or relent. Like the poisonous poppies in *The Wizard of Oz*, this field deceives you with its beauty and ease till you're overcome with sin's deadly scent. The world walks defiantly hand-in-hand through this field declaring a better, more tolerant, and wiser way than God's while deceiving themselves with every comfortable step and marching closer to their own demise.

The constant pressure of our circumstances and the antagonism we face from others puts us in great straits (G4712)—trouble, distress, and pain. We believers will never be free from this while we breathe. It is human nature to run far from sorrow and affliction, but thanks be to our Lord, Jesus Christ, He chose to be straitened *by* it. "But I have a baptism to be baptized with; and how am I straitened till it be accomplished!" (Luke 12:50). He chose to place His love for us above His suffering and anguish so we could be genuinely free.

Our Christian walk is fraught with straits. Like a steep mountain gorge with crumbling walls on either side, this is no comfy trek. But we can help each other over the rough spots with a steady shoulder and a prayer, beckoning those behind us and cheering on those ahead. But even if you're alone on this trail longing for support, remember there's a guardrail the whole way. Hold on tightly to Christ and you will get to the top.

When thou goest, thy steps shall not be straitened; and when thou runnest, thou shalt not stumble.
(Proverbs 4:12)

17

Strive

*And the servant of the Lord must not **strive**; but be gentle unto all men, apt to teach, patient. (2 Timothy 2:24)*

*Now I beseech you, brethren, for the Lord Jesus Christ's sake, and for the love of the Spirit, that ye **strive** together with me in your prayers to God for me. (Romans 15:30)*

As we sit in the quiet or blessed chaos of our days to study our KJV Bibles, we might come across seeming contradictions in the words that are used. In one place we are told we should not strive, and in another, we are told we should. So, which is it? To strive or not to strive, that is the question.

The word *strive* in the KJV means different things in different situations when applied to God, other people, mental activity, or physical things. When we strive or fight amongst ourselves, physically or verbally (H7378; G3164), if we wrangle over superficial doctrinal issues or other

Strive

H1777 *dîn*; to *rule*; to *judge* (as umpire), also to *strive* (as at law):— to contend, execute judgment, judge, minister judgment, plead, plead the cause, at strife

H7378 *rîb*; to *toss*, i.e. *grapple*; figuratively to *wrangle*, i.e. *hold a controversy*; (by implication) to *defend*:— adversary, chide, complain, contend, debate, lay wait, plead, rebuke

H5327 *nâṣâ*; properly to *go forth*, i.e. (by implication) to *be expelled*, and (consequently) *desolate*; causatively to *lay waste*, (specifically) to *quarrel*:— be laid waste, ruinous, strive together

H3401 *yârîb*; literally *he will contend*; properly *contentious*, used as noun, an *adversary*:— that contend, that strive

G2051 *erizō* to *wrangle*:— strive

G75 *agōnizomai*; to *struggle*, literally (to *compete* for a prize), figuratively (to *contend* with an adversary); or generally (to *endeavor* to accomplish something):— fight, labor fervently

G4865 *synagōnizomai*; to *struggle* in company *with*; i.e. (figuratively) to *be a partner* (assistant):— to strive together with

G118 *athleō*; (a *contest* in the public lists); to *contend* in the competitive games:— strive

G3054 *logomacheō*; to *be disputatious* (on trifles):— strive about words

G3164 *machmai*; to *war*; i.e. (figuratively) to *quarrel*, *dispute*:— fight

Strived G5389 *pholotimeomai*; to be *fond of honor*, i.e. *emulous* (*eager* or *earnest* to do something):— labour, strive, study

Striven H1624 *gārā*; properly to *grate*, i.e. (figuratively) to *anger*:— contend, meddle, stir up

Striveth H7378 and G75: see definitions above

Striving G75: see definition above

G464 *antagōnizomai*; to *struggle against* (figuratively) [*"antagonize"*]:— strive against

G4866 *synathleō*; to *wrestle* in company *with*; (figuratively) to *seek jointly*:— labour with, strive together for

Strivings H7379 *rîb* from H7378; a *contest* (personal or legal):— adversary

inconsequential things, or worst yet, if we strive with God Himself, this is the kind of striving the Bible warns us against.

In daily life, we strive over many trivial and unimportant things (but oh, how they matter in the moment!). We are all guilty of making mountains out of molehills. It takes intentional growing as sons and daughters of the most high God to get past the angst that makes us strive wrongfully.

> Strive not with a man without cause, if he have done thee no harm. (Proverbs 3:30)

> Go not forth hastily to strive, lest thou know not what to do in the end thereof, when thy neighbour hath put thee to shame. (Proverbs 25:8)

The apostle Paul spoke to Timothy about the desire many in the church had to debate back and forth about issues that ultimately had no bearing on their salvation and, essentially, were a waste of time. This is still true today. One debate within the Christian community is the pre-tribulation rapture. Although Scripture doesn't explicitly support it (read Matthew 24:29–31; 1 Corinthians 15:22–23; and 1 Thessalonians 4:15–17), why fight about who's right? We'll find out soon enough, and then what? Will the pre- or post-tribbers taunt "I told you so!" to their fellow brethren? That doesn't sound very Christ-like, now does it?

> *Neither give heed to fables and endless genealogies, which minister questions, rather than godly edifying which is in faith: so do. (1 Timothy 1:4)*

> *Of these things put them in remembrance, charging them before the Lord that they strive not about words to no profit, but to the subverting of the hearers. (2 Timothy 2:14)*

Getting worked up over issues that don't matter spiritually defiles us. Opinions vary, especially among women, as to what is or isn't right for a Christian. Short hair or long, pants or skirts, home school or public, stay-at-home or work outside the home, smoking, drinking, piercings, head coverings, KJV only or modern translations, and the list goes on and on. Although there may be scriptural proof to back up what you think about these issues, if what you argue for or against causes doubt in a new believer or isn't relevant to salvation, there's no benefit to this kind of striving. It only divides the body of Christ. But if we see a sister follow a spiritual matter incorrectly, gentle words spoken with love should be our approach, not striving. Because we all have much to learn. And none of us knows it all. God works with each person at his or her own pace for their learning and overcoming. He is patient, but we, often, are not.

> *Hast thou faith? have it to thyself before God. Happy is he that condemneth not himself in that thing which he alloweth. (Romans 14:22)*

> *But avoid foolish questions, and genealogies, and contentions, and strivings about the law; for they are unprofitable and vain. (Titus 3:9)*

Because we go through different stages of growth in our Christian calling, what we allow for ourselves now may change, as our understanding of God's truth matures. Our beliefs shouldn't ever be based on the prevailing consensus, but on what God has revealed to us through His Word. Are our convictions based on faith or peer-pressure? Because if it is not by faith, it is sin (Romans 14:23).

> *Woe unto him that striveth with his Maker! Let the potsherd strive with the potsherds of the earth. Shall the clay say to him that fashioneth it, What makest thou? or thy work, He hath no hands? (Isaiah 45:9)*

Who would strive against the Lord God? How is that even done? The obvious way is by actively working against good and promoting evil, as governments around the world do. To strive against God is not only foolish but frightening. It is a fearful thing to fall into the hands of the living God (Hebrews 10:31).

> *Behold, all they that were incensed against* [God]
> *shall be ashamed and confounded: they shall be as*
> *nothing; and they that strive with thee shall perish.*
> *(Isaiah 41:11)*

Do you strive (H7378 *grapple, contend, complain, hold a controversy*) with God without realizing it? If you question God's righteous judgment over matters you haven't fully accepted like divorce, homosexuality, submission to a husband, forgiveness, obedience, self-sacrifice, etc., you strive with your Maker. And we've all done it. When we want our lives to go a certain way, to fit our preconceived parameter of what we think is right, but it goes against what God already said is right, we strive with our Maker. Sadly, many Christian churches strive with God when they accept the world's standards and invite those standards to traipse through their aisles and defile the minds of their congregation.

> *Fight the good fight of faith, lay hold on eternal life,*
> *whereunto thou art also called, and hast professed a*
> *good profession before many witnessed.*
> *(1 Timothy 6:12)*

There is a *good* fight—the fight of faith. A time to strive for something noble and right. The meaning of fight in 1 Timothy 6:12 means the same thing as the word *strive* (G75) in Luke 13:24 when Christ tells us to strive to enter the strait gate. It means to struggle, to compete for a prize, to contend with an adversary, to endeavor or accomplish something, to fight or labor fervently. But why must we fight for our faith? Because the devil doesn't want us to win the war or realize its importance. He wants lazy, unprepared Christians who think they don't need to do anything after conversion. Satan can easily fool these people and render their faith inert, powerless, empty because they aren't grasping onto it fiercely.

Remember in Philippians 2:12 where we are told to "work out your own salvation with fear and trembling"? Our Christian calling is not a passive one. We are encouraged to ardently finish what God started in us. But how do we do this? By following Paul's example to "press toward the mark for the prize of the high calling of God in Christ Jesus" (Philippians 3:14) with our obedience, repentance, and perseverance.

> *Whereunto I also labour, striving according to his working, which worketh in me mightily.*
> *(Colossians 1:19)*

Paul encouraged active, purposeful striving for the only thing that truly matters in this life: to hear these glorious words, "Well done, thou good and faithful servant" at Christ's return.

"And if a man also strive for masteries, yet is he not crowned, except he strive lawfully" (2 Timothy 2:5) There is lawful and unlawful striving. Like Martha, who was troubled by all she put upon herself to do, we strive in ways that hinder our peace and blind us from the needful thing. You might work tirelessly to write meaningful books, gather crowds from a stage, run a stellar business, offer a spotless house of hospitality all from the standpoint of wanting to be known, loved, and sought after. But what good are these gleaming trophies if you lose your soul (Mark 8:36)? Yet if you strive for mastery over your carnal self, there's a crown of life waiting for you, an eternal accolade (1 Corinthians 9:25; James 1:12; Revelation 2:10).

It doesn't matter if you lack talent or beauty or charm to impress, or whether you live up to anyone else's standards. God looks at the inner man, the contrite heart, the "weak" and "foolish" to confound the mighty and wise (1 Corinthians 1:27). We are chosen and royal and holy to God (1 Peter 2:9) because we have chosen to obey our King in our most holy faith.

Only let your conversation be as it becometh the gospel of Christ . . . that ye stand fast in one spirit, with one mind striving together for the faith of the gospel. (Philippians 1:27)

When we strive together (G4866) in faith and prayer, we become partners with our fellow brothers and sisters, near and far, and our hidden work builds up the body of Christ and brings about unity in the Spirit that pleases God.

Lastly, let us strive to enter that most difficult of gates spoken of by our King and Savior, Jesus Christ. "Strive to enter in at the strait gate: for many, I say unto you, will seek to enter in, and shall not be able" (Luke 13:24). Entering this intentionally limited passageway takes great effort, unlike the wide gate the world offers. Their conduit is all-inclusive; it doesn't require you to change. It is contrary to God and embraces evil unabashedly. But uproarious joy is ours at Christ's return if we follow God's mandate to strive (G75 *labor fervently, struggle, fight*) to get through His gate and walk the narrow road that leads to life with Him.

There is only one occurrence of the H1777 definition of strive where God strives with man. In Genesis 6:3 He says, "My spirit shall not always strive with man, for that he also is flesh: yet his days shall be an hundred and twenty years." *Strive* here means to "rule, judge, contend, and plead with." This verse makes two points: (1) God put a cap on our physical lifespan, and (2) God won't be dealing with us as weak and faulted human beings forever. No longer will we need judgment or ruling as wayward children need. We will have stepped past the threshold of limitations on our mortal selves, and the sin that so easily besets us (Hebrews 12:1), and into the grand expanse of immortality where we will be like God, righteous and true. What joy!

Beloved, now are we the sons of God, and it doth not yet appear what we shall be: but we know that, when he shall appear, we shall be like him; for we shall see him as he is. (1 John 3:2)

[18]

Succour

*For in that he himself hath suffered being tempted, he is able to **succour** them that are tempted. (Hebrews 2:18)*

Imagine you are strolling a field of waving grasses when you inadvertently slip into a deep and slimy pit where temptation had lain hidden. Your feet can't touch bottom, the sludge weighs you down and mire, thick with rotting vegetation, closes in around your face. You raise your head spitting muck from your mouth and shout in fear for help, for someone to rescue you from a horrible death.

Just then a sturdy rope appears tied to an immovable object you had not seen before, and with trembling arms and racing heart, you haul yourself out and lie quivering on the green, tears of relief spilling from your tightly closed eyes. Jesus Christ, our Rock unmoved, our willing Rescuer, longs to save us from the imminent doom of this suffocating quicksand world, if we would but reach for His hand.

Succour

H5826 *āzar*; to *surround*, i.e. *protect* or *aid*:— help

G997 *boētheō* from G998; to *aid* or *relieve*:— help

Succoured H5826: see definition above

G997: see definition above

Succourer G4368 *prostatis*; a *patroness*, i.e. *assistant*:— succourer

Help G997: see definition above

G996 *boētheia* taken from G998; *aid*; specifically a rope or chain for *securing* a vessel:— help

Helper G998 *bēothos*; (to *run*); a *rescuer*:— helper

G997: see definition above

From *Merriam-Webster's Collegiate Dictionary*:

succor: to give assistance to in time of need or distress

For I the Lord thy God will hold thy right hand,
saying unto thee, Fear not; I will help thee.
(Isaiah 41:13)

In our most fearful and debilitating moments, we cry out to God for deliverance. Who but God can surround us with His mighty angels, protect us from the wickedness that exists around us, and fill us with His Spirit to crush the wickedness from within us? God has promised to surround, protect, and give us His aid. Fear not, indeed!

The word *succour* (pronounced *sucker*) is used three times in the Old Testament and two in the New. Since the words *succour* (H5826; G997) and *help* (H5826; G997) both come from the same Hebrew or Greek root word, the translators of the KJV Bible often interchanged them, as they did in Isaiah 41 and in the Psalms below.

And the Lord shall help them, and deliver them: he
shall deliver them from the wicked, and save them,
because they trust in him. (Psalm 37:40)

Help us, O God of our salvation, for the glory of thy
name: and deliver us, and purge away our sins, for
thy name's sake. (Psalm 79:9)

If you are a parent, the story of a father's immense love for his sick child in Mark chapter 9 hits our hearts hard. Like him, we've often begged God for compassion, for the help we so desperately needed in our hopeless situations. But reading this man's distraught last remarks to our Lord can't help but prick tears because we know the truth that lies behind it.

> *And ofttimes it hath cast him into the fire, and into the waters, to destroy him: but if thou canst do any thing, have compassion on us, and help us.*
> *Jesus said unto him, If you canst believe, all things are possible to him that believeth.*
> *And straightway the father of the child cried out, and said with tears, Lord, I believe; help thou mine unbelief. (Mark 9:22–24)*

Help thou mine unbelief! Oh, yes, do we not struggle like this father to be ever faithful? To never waver? We cry out to God with the same desperate plea: *We believe you, Lord, please help us when we let faith slip.* We need Christ's lifeline to rescue us from the faithlessness that clings to our fears. The word *help* in Mark 9 verse 22 comes from the same Greek word *boetheo* (G997) as *succour* does.

There are quite a few women in the Bible to admire: Sarah, Deborah, Esther, Ruth. They each have godly qualities that we would do well to emulate. But Phoebe, whom Paul mentioned in Romans 16, is often overlooked.

> *I commend unto you Phēbe our sister, which is a servant of the church which is at Cenchrea:*
> *That you receive her in the Lord, as becometh saints, and that ye assist her in whatsoever business she hath need of you: for she hath been a succourer of many, and of myself also. (Romans 16:1–2)*

Sister, servant, saint, and succorer of many. What a beautiful tribute Paul gave her. Although the apostle Paul gave Phoebe (spelled *Phebe* in Greek) this dignified title, he could have used the common word "helper," but he recognized her service was far more than that. Succourer (G4368) comes from the Greek noun *prostatis*. According to *Vine's Complete Expository Dictionary*, the word *prostatēs* (and the feminine variant *prostatis*) was the title of a citizen of Athens who had the responsibility of seeing to the welfare of resident aliens who were without civic rights.

By this definition, Phoebe was a protectress. She had wealth and influence and used these advantages not for her own benefit, but for the benefit of her Christian brethren, taking on the responsibility to support their needs. Although the Bible does not explicitly say, Phoebe was most likely a single woman. Married women are spoken for, time-wise. As you know, we cannot be everywhere and be all things to all people. Our mission as wives and mothers is to give ourselves to our families first, then to our friends, businesses, and ministries. Instead of pouring herself out for a husband and children, Phoebe poured herself out for the children of God. She used her resources—time, money, and a servant's heart—to bless her church family. She made it her business to be available and to love them well.

When you give your precious time and energy to make a meal for a shut-in, send a get-well card to a sick member of your church, babysit for that exhausted mom, or say a prayer for a hurting friend while listening to her grieve, you are doing more than mere helping. You are giving them much-needed relief. You are being a Phoebe.

We may not be able to succor with the same singleness of heart as Phoebe did for the church, but we can still be a "succourer of many" at home. Our husbands need us to protect our children from the evil that creeps into their lives via peers and entertainment and their own selfish attitudes. They need us to protect our marriages and guard our hearts by using social media wisely and speaking about them respectfully to others when they're not in the room. We need to be, as Phoebe was to the church, the best assistant they could ask for.

Before the foundation of the world, God made a way for us to live eternally with Him. That way was His Son who willingly sacrificed Himself for the joy set before Him. We are that joy!

For we have not an high priest which cannot be touched with the feeling of our infirmities; but was in all points tempted like as we are, yet without sin. Let us therefore come boldly unto the throne of grace, that we may obtain mercy, and find grace to help in time of need. (Hebrews 4:15–16)

The divine Christ lowered Himself to embody the weakness of man that through death He could destroy him who had the power over death, our adversary, the devil. Christ, born flesh and blood like us, understands our multitude of sufferings, our manifold temptations, having lived through them Himself. He knows our pain and is perfectly willing to carry us up and out of the world's smothering confines if we but surrender our lives to Him (Hebrews 2:18).

For he saith, I have heard thee in a time accepted,
and in the day of salvation have I succoured thee:
behold, now is the accepted time; behold, now is the
day of salvation. (2 Corinthians 6:2)

God has saved us through Christ. He has succored us
with the hope found only in His name. Now is the time,
dear women. Your salvation bound securely to Christ is
right in front of you. Grab onto it for dear life.

Wist/Wit/Wot

*And when the children of Israel saw it, they said one to another, it is manna: for they **wist not** what it was. (Exodus 16:15)*

*That every man should let his manservant, and every man his maidservant, being an Hebrew or an Hebrewess, go free; that none should serve himself of them, **to wit**, of a Jew his brother. (Jeremiah 34:9)*

*And now, brethren, **I wot** that through ignorance ye did it, as did also your rulers. (Acts 3:17)*

Wist, wit, wot: These three odd words used in the King James Version are not as complicated as they seem if we exchange them in our heads with modern equivalents as we read the text. In the Old Testament, the meaning of all instances of *wist*, *wit*, and *wot* have the same etymological origin. They all come from the Hebrew word

Wist

H3045 *yāda*; to *know* (properly to ascertain by *seeing*); used in a variety of senses, figurative and literal (including *observation, care, recognition* and *instruction, designation, punishment*):— acknowledge, advise answer, be aware, unawares, comprehend, consider, be diligent, discern, discover, make known, be learned, mark, perceive, privy to, man of skill, be sure, teach, understand, have understanding

G1492 *eidō*; properly to *see* (literally or figuratively); to *know*:— be aware, behold, can (+ not tell), consider, know, have knowledge, look (on), perceive, be sure, tell, understand, wish

Wit

H3045: see definition above

G5613 *hōs*; *which how,* i.e. *in that manner:*— about, after that, (according) as (it had been, it were), like unto, how (greatly), since, so that, whensoever, while, with all speed

G1107 *gnōrizō*; to *make known*; subject to *know:*— certify, declare, make know, give to understand, do to wit, wot

Wot

H3045: see definition above

G1492: see definition above

G1107: see definition above

yada meaning to "know" or to "see" in various applications whether literally or figuratively.

Wist not (wist is always paired with not) means "did not know." The phrase *to wit*, always with its obligatory "to" in front of it, means to know, or to acknowledge that something is, or to discover what something will be. But it can also mean *according as it were, that is, how*, and *since*.

Wot not is similar to wist not in that it means to "not know" or to "not see" (figuratively), to "not be sure" of something. Grammatically, *wit* and *wist* are the past tense verb forms of *wot*. Of the ten times wot is used, eight are *wot not's* and two are simply *wot*. Let us explore some examples of these words as they are used in the King James Version:

> *And when the children of Israel saw it, they said one to another, it is manna: for they wist not what it was. And Moses said unto them, This is the bread which the Lord hath given you to eat.*
> *(Exodus 16:15)*

The twelve tribes of Israel were given a gift from heaven, something completely unusual they had never seen before. They had no idea what it was. Hence, the word *manna* means "whatness" or "what!" with its exclamation point.

> *And it came to pass, when Moses came down from mount Sinai with the two tables of testimony in Moses' hand, when he came down from the mount, that Moses wist not that the skin of his face shone while he talked with him. (Exodus 34:29)*

Moses didn't realize his face was glowing from the encounter with the glory of the Lord. It was such a frightening and awesome sight (in the truest sense of the word) that the people compelled Moses to cover his face with a veil when he spoke to them. They just couldn't handle it, and if this incident happened today, we'd be a little unsettled too.

Continuing on with *wist*, in Luke 2:49, the young Jesus tells his exasperated, three-days-searching-for-him parents, "How is it that ye sought me? wist ye not that I must be about my Father's business?" He tells them plainly, *Why were you looking for me? Didn't you know I have my Father's work to do?* After three, long, probably frantic days, can you imagine the looks Joseph and Mary gave to each other after hearing this?

> *And there appeared unto them Elias* [Elijah] *with Moses: and they were talking with Jesus. And Peter answered and said to Jesus, Master, it is good for us to be here: and let us make three tabernacles; one for thee, and one for Moses, and one for Elias.*
> *For he wist not what to say; for they were sore afraid. (Mark 9:5–6)*

How many of us find ourselves unsure of what to say, but we blabber on anyway? Peter was an impulsive soul and often spoke or did things before thinking. But it's always better to wait before speaking about things we don't understand. Ecclesiastes 5:2 says, "Be not rash with thy mouth, and let not thine heart be hasty to utter any thing before God: for God is in heaven, and thou upon earth: therefore let thy words be few." James 1:19 says it this way, "Wherefore, my beloved brethren, let every man be swift to hear, slow to speak, slow to wrath."

In Acts 12:9, after defying the ruler's demand to stop proclaiming Christ, Peter thought he was dreaming when his chains fell off, and he was led right out of the prison cell by an angel. This miraculous scene would have seemed like a dream to us, too, if we had been in his place.

> *And he went out, and followed him; and wist not that it was true which was done by the angel; but thought he saw a vision. (Acts 12:9)*

> *Then said Paul, I wist not, brethren, that he was the high priest: for it is written, Thou shalt not speak evil of the ruler of thy people. (Acts 23:5)*

In this last example of *wist*, Paul was being facetious with his use of the phrase after he was struck in the face by a councilman on the order of the high priest. If Paul were speaking now, he'd say: "I wish he weren't the high priest because we're not supposed to say bad things about our leaders, but this guy deserves it!"

Now onto the second word: (to) *wit*. Abraham's servant, who was sent on a mission to find a wife for his master's son, Isaac, waited and didn't say anything right away or do anything hasty until he was "to wit" or *sure* that the woman in front of him (that is, Rebekah) was indeed the right woman God intended for Isaac.

And the man wondering at her held his peace, to wit
whether the Lord had made his journey prosperous
or not. (Genesis 24:21)

And his sister stood afar off, to wit what would be
done to him. (Exodus 2:4)

In Exodus, we read that young Miriam waited in the
reeds *to wit* or to discover what would happen to her baby
brother, Moses, as she watched Pharaoh's daughter's servants
draw the basket from the water that held him.

There are only two instances of *to wit* in the New
Testament. Both are found in 2 Corinthians and both have
different meanings:

Moreover, brethren, we do you to wit [G1107, we
certify and want you to know] *of the grace of God*
bestowed on the churches of Macedonia.
(2 Corinthians 8:1)

And all things are of God, who hath reconciled us to
himself by Jesus Christ, and hath given to us the
ministry of reconciliation;
To wit [G5613, how, according as it were, since],
that God was in Christ, reconciling the world unto
himself, not imputing their trespasses unto them; and
hath committed unto us the word of reconciliation.
(2 Corinthians 5:18–19)

And lastly, we have *wot*. In Acts 7:40, Stephen quoted from Exodus 32 to the angry crowd in Jerusalem, reminding them of their history and disobedience to God, "Saying unto Aaron, make us gods to go before us: for as for this Moses, which brought us out of the land of Egypt, we wot not what is become of him." The children of Israel didn't have much patience or faith in their God even though He had fashioned a divine escape from the Egyptian army for them through the Red Sea. Since Moses was taking so long on Mount Sinai, and they *wot not* or didn't know what happened to him, they decided to take matters into their own hands.

Paul referred to 1 Kings 19 and the story of Elijah distraught in his cave when he spoke to the Roman church. "God hath not cast away his people which he foreknew. Wot ye not [don't you know] what the scripture saith of Elias?" (Romans 11:2, emphasis added). When things look their bleakest, when it seems we are all alone in this evil world, there is always hope. God intimately knew and protected every one of the faithful who had not defiled themselves with other gods in Elijah's time, and He does and will do the same for us now.

> For to me to live is Christ, and to die is gain. But if I live in the flesh, this is the fruit of my labour: yet what I shall choose I wot not. (Philippians 1:22)

By the time Paul wrote the epistle to the Philippians, he was tired. He had been through a lot and longed for the rest that would be revealed at his very next moment of consciousness after death. But he also knew that his calling was to serve the brethren, and he didn't want to leave them. Serving Christ was his joy while in the flesh. But he knew even more joy awaited him after death. He was "betwixt two" choices and *wot not* what to choose, wanting to stay alive for the benefit of those he served, but also sleep in death so he could be in the presence of Christ when he and the faithful are resurrected at Christ's return (See Colossians 3:4; 2 Timothy 4:8; and 1 Peter 5:4).

How many of us who've been long on this earth feel the same way? We're tired. We want it to be over—the pain (physical and mental), the difficulties left and right, the mocking of God's truth, and the persecution of His elect. Life is hard. It was hard then, and it's hard now. But Christ was with Paul and the faithful in Paul's day, and Christ is with us now in ours. We have nothing to fear. We can be certain that our lives are in the palm of the Father's hand, and His love will guide and protect us till our very last breath.

And we know that the Son of God is come, and hath given us an understanding, that we may know him that is true, and we are in him that is true, even in his Son Jesus Christ. This is the true God, and eternal life. (1 John 5:20)

[20]

Bonus Words

The following words did not have enough material to be given their own chapters but still need some spotlighting to address any confusion these unusual words present in our reading of the King James Version.

20. Behoved

G1163 *dei*, also *deon*; it is (*was*) *necessary* (as *binding*):— must (needs), need, be needful, ought, should
G3784 *opheilō*; to *owe* (monetarily); figuratively to *be under obligation*; morally to fail in duty:— be bound, debt, due, duty, be guilty (indebted), must needs, ought

> And said unto them, "Thus it is written, and thus it behoved Christ to suffer, and to rise from the dead the third day:
> And that repentance and remission of sins should be preached in his name among all nations, beginning at Jerusalem." (Luke 24:46–47)

*Wherefore in all things it behoved him to be made
like unto his brethren, that he might be a merciful
and faithful high priest in things pertaining to God,
to make reconciliation for the sins of the people.
(Hebrews 2:17)*

As already covered in the study of the word *perfect* and
mentioned again for the word *propitiation* (in this bonus
words chapter), without Christ's willing sacrifice, we would
have no path to eternal life, no forgiveness of sins.
Thankfully, Christ chose to suffer the agony and indignity
of the cross. Both instances of the word *behoved* found in the
New Testament speak about Christ and what was *necessary*
for Him to intercede on our behave. He took on the form
of flesh and blood mankind to experience our temptations
firsthand so He could be the consummate comforter, and
then He willingly and obediently laid it down. He was
bound by His love for us to do so.

Chambering

G2845 *koitē*; a *couch*; by extension *cohabitation*; by
implication the male *sperm*:— bed, conceive

Used once in the New Testament, chambering is illicit
intercourse, the modern-day equivalent of "sleeping
around." Yikes. Some things never change.

*Let us walk honestly, as in the day; not in rioting and
drunkenness, not in chambering and wantonness,
not in strife and envying. (Romans 13:13)*

Concupiscence

G1939 *epithymia*; a *longing* (especially for what is forbidden):— desire, lust after

This odd word is found three times in the New Testament. A synonym of *lust*, concupiscence is taken from G1937 which means to set the *heart upon*, to *long for* something rightfully or otherwise. But concupiscence is a desire for something you cannot rightfully have, something illicit, as Paul spoke in Romans, "But sin, taking occasion by the commandment, wrought in me all manner of concupiscence. For without the law sin was dead" (Romans 7:8). See also Colossians 3:5 and 1 Thessalonians 4:5

Condescend

G4879 *synopagō*; to *take off together*, i.e. *transport with* (*seduce*, passive *yield*):— carry (lead) away with

We are most familiar with the *Merriam-Webster's* definition of *condescend* and *condescension* meaning "to assume an air of superiority" and "to exhibit a patronizing attitude or behavior." But *condescend* in the KJV (used once in the New Testament), means to be carried away or to allow yourself to yield to what might seem "beneath" you. "Be of the same mind one toward another. Mind not high things, but condescend to men of low estate. Be not wise in your own conceits" (Romans 12:16).

In the marginal notes for *condescend* in Romans 12:16, we find the phrase "be contented with mean things." *Mean things* are common, mediocre, everyday things, the opposite of high and lofty things. When we "condescend" the KJV way, we let ourselves be carried away with fellow brethren like us, common everyday believers who cannot superficially increase our status or reputation. This is one way we show our love.

Convenient

H2706 *ḥōq*; an *enactment*; hence an *appointment*:— appointed, bound, due, measure

H3477 *yāśār*; *straight* (literally or figuratively):— equity, meet, just, upright

G2119 *eukaireō*; to *have good time*, i.e. opportunity or leisure:— spend time

G2520 *kathēkō*; to *reach to*, i.e. becoming:— fit

G2540 *kairos*; an *occasion*, i.e. *set* or *proper* time:— due season, due time, a while

G433 *anēkō*; to *attain to*, i.e. (figuratively) *be proper*:— be fit

Convenient means what we think it means in most of the entries in the KJV: well-timed and appropriate for ease and advantage. But there are a couple of uses that differ.

In Romans 1:28, "And even as they did not like to retain God in their knowledge, God gave them over to a reprobate mind, to do those things which are not convenient (G2520)." Here the worldly are engaging in activity that is *unbecoming* of a creation of God.

In Ephesians 5:4, "Neither filthiness, nor foolish talking, nor jesting, which are not convenient (G433): but rather giving of thanks." These actions are not *fit* for a Christian to engage in.

And in Philemon:

Wherefore, though I might be much bold in Christ to enjoin thee that which is convenient [G433], *Yet for love's sake I rather beseech thee, being such an one as Paul the aged, and now also a prisoner of Jesus Christ. (Philemon 8–9)*

Paul could have commanded Philemon to do that which was proper, but wanted him to choose what love would do instead.

Dissimulation

G505 *anypokritos*; *not dissembled*, i.e. *sincere:*— without hypocrisy, unfeigned

G5272 *hypokrisis*; *acting under* a feigned part, i.e. (figuratively) *deceit:*— condemnation, hypocrisy

The word *dissimulation* (G5272) is a close cousin to the words *dissemble* and *feign* which mean to "pretend," or to "play the hypocrite." Dissimulation is equal to hypocrisy. Now add "without" to dissimulation and you get the G505 definition, which is the opposite and means *sincere*.

"Let love be without dissimulation. Abhor that which is evil; cleave to that which is good" (Romans 12:9). Our fulfillment of godly love—"unfeigned love of the brethren" (1 Peter 1:22)—must always be true, sincere, without any hypocrisy or falsehood or hopes of gaining an advantage.

For before that certain came from James, he [Peter]
did eat with the Gentiles: but when they were come,
he withdrew and separated himself, fearing them
which were of the circumcision.
And the other Jews dissembled likewise with him;
insomuch that Barnabas also was carried away with
their dissimulation. (Galatians 2:12–13)

Instead of standing his ground and doing the right thing, Peter feared what the Pharisees would think of him and thus became a hypocrite (and influenced others likewise), acting a certain way to a certain crowd one moment and then playing a different character the next. Fear of offending others sometimes makes us act shamefully, but fear of offending God should be the stronger drive. Let us women strive to be true in everything we do. "But the wisdom that is from above is first pure, then peaceable, gentle, and easy to be intreated, full of mercy and good fruits, without partiality, and without hypocrisy" (James 3:17).

Emulation-Emulations

G2205 *zēlos*; properly *heat*, i.e. (figuratively) *"zeal"* (in a favorable sense *ardor*; in an unfavorable sense, *jealousy*, as of a husband [figuratively of God]):— envy, fervent mind, indignation

G3863 *parazēloō*; to *stimulate along side*, i.e. *excite to rivalry*:— provoke to jealousy

"If by any means I may provoke to emulation (G3863) them which are my flesh, and might save some of them"

(Romans 11:14). Used in a righteous sense, Paul hoped to stir the hearts of his fellow countrymen with godly jealousy to pursue their savior, Jesus Christ, as the Gentiles he had taught were doing humbly and joyfully.

"Now the works of the flesh are . . . Idolatry, witchcraft, hatred, variance, emulations (G2205), wrath, strife, seditions, heresies . . ." (Galatians 5:19–20). In this long list of works of the flesh, emulations conveys wrongful jealousy, envy, or indignation we must cast aside if we want to inherit the coming kingdom of God.

Endued

H2064 *zābad*; to *confer:*— endue
H3045 *yāda*; to *know:*— endued with
G1746 *endyō*; (in the sense of *sinking* into a garment), to *invest* with clothing:— array, clothe with, endue, have (put) on
G1990 *epistēmōn*; *intelligent:*— endued with knowledge

> *And, behold, I send the promise of my Father upon you: but tarry ye in the city of Jerusalem, until ye be endued with power from on high. (Luke 24:49)*

> *Who is a wise man and endued with knowledge among you? let him shew out of a good conversation his works with meekness of wisdom. (James 3:13)*

In all four examples of *endue*, found twice in the Old Testament, twice in the New, it is God who is giving a gift: conception for Leah (Genesis 30:20), wisdom and knowledge for Solomon (2 Chronicles 2:12), and the Holy Spirit Christ promised to send from the Father upon our conversion (Luke 24:49).

Endued is a wrapping, a garment that covers or envelops us. The apostle Paul spoke in 1 Corinthians 15:53 about us needing to "put on" immortality (G1746 *endue*) as we cannot wear our old clothes in the kingdom. He expounded upon this concept in 2 Corinthians 5:2–4 when he said we earnestly wait "to be clothed upon" (again G1746), to finally shed this tiresome mortal cloth and be wrapped in righteous immortality.

The word *endue* is closely synonymous with the words *imbue* (to permeate, transfuse) and *endow* (to provide, furnish with a gift). At the resurrection, we will rise endowed with the gift of white linen woven in love and mercy and honor, fully imbued with the Spirit as we are changed into spirit. We will be arrayed in eternity as we look with elation upon the face of God.

Froward

H8419 *tahpūkâ*; a *perversity* or *fraud*:— perverse thing
H6141 *iqqēš*; *distorted*; hence *false*:— crooked, perverse
H6617 *pātal*; to *twine*, i.e. (literally) to *struggle* or (figuratively) *be* (morally) *tortuous*:— shew thyself unsavoury, wrestle
H3868 *lûz*; to *turn* aside, i.e. (literally) to *depart*, (figuratively) *be perverse*:— perverseness
H6143 *iqqĕšût*; *perversity*:— froward
G4646 *skolios*; *warped*, i.e. *winding*; figuratively *perverse*:— crooked, untoward

And he [God] *said, I will hide my face from them, I will see what their end shall be: for they are a very froward generation, children in whom is no faith. (Deuteronomy 32:20)*

They that are of a froward heart are abomination to the Lord: but such as are upright in their way are his delight. (Proverbs 11:20)

Anyone we surround ourselves with who has a froward (H6141 *false, crooked*) heart, even a loved one, has the potential to negatively influence our Christian walk. "A froward heart shall depart from me: I will not know a wicked person" (Psalm 101:4). The psalmist's admonition to steer clear of these people is especially hard for us women. We often don't want to appear judgmental or cause a disturbance, so we try to get along with unbelieving family and friends. But no good will come from tolerating sinful behavior. Eventually, we will have to separate ourselves from them for our spiritual sanity.

"And with many other words did he testify and exhort, saying, Save yourselves from this untoward generation" (Acts 2:40). In this verse, the word *untoward* (G4646, used once in the KJV) is identical in meaning to *froward.* Peter told us to save ourselves, or preserve or keep ourselves safe from the influence of our increasingly perverse and warped society. Never more true than today. "That ye may be blameless and harmless, the sons of God, without rebuke, in the midst of a crooked (G4646) and perverse nation, among whom ye shine as lights in the world" (Philippians 2:15).

Horn

H7161 *qeren*; a *horn* (as projecting); by implication a *flask*, *cornet*; by resemblance an elephant's *tooth* (ivory), a *corner* (of the altar), a *peak* (of a mountain), a *ray* (of light); figuratively *power*:— hill

H7162 *qeren* (Aramaic) corresponding to H7161; a *horn* (literally or for sound):— cornet [musical instrument]

G2768 *keras*; (the *hair* of the head); a *horn* (literal or figurative):— horn

The word *horn* can mean a physical projection on the head of a beast (Daniel 7:7–8) or the musical instrument projecting sound, as in a trumpet (Joshua 6:5). But what might confuse us is when horn is used symbolically as in, "He also exalteth the horn of his people, the praise of all his saints; even of the children of Israel, a people near unto him. Praise ye the Lord" (Psalm 148:14).

For these instances, horn means the strength or power we possess, and when linked with the word *salvation*, means the peak of purpose, the point (without any pun intended) for our being born.

> *The Lord is my rock, and my fortress, and my deliverer; my God, my strength, in whom I will trust; my buckler, and the horn of my salvation, and my high tower. (Psalm 18:2).*

Incontinency-Incontinent

G192 *akrasia*; *want of self-restraint*:— excess

G193 *akratēs*; *powerless*, i.e. *without self-control*:— incontinent

This is not a bladder leakage problem we're talking about here (although "incontinence products" makes sense now, doesn't it?). *Incontinency*, the two times the word is used in the New Testament, means "not controlling our actions and emotions, lacking self-control."

> *Defraud ye not one the other, except it be with consent for a time, that ye may give yourselves to fasting and prayer; and come together again, that Satan tempt you not for your incontinency.*
> *(1 Corinthians 7:5)*

A marriage needs sexual intimacy. So, when a husband and wife abstain for a time because of sickness, or travel, or busy life events, it must not last too long. Otherwise, temptations that marriage was designed to alleviate have the potential to crop up where there were none. Incontinency—a lack of self-restraint, an inability to control wandering thoughts—leads to sin.

> *For men shall be lovers of their own selves, covetous, boasters, proud, blasphemers, disobedient to parents, unthankful, unholy,*
> *Without natural affection, trucebreakers, false accusers, incontinent, fierce, despisers of those that are good,*
> *Traitors, heady, highminded, lovers of pleasures more than lovers of God. (2 Timothy 3:2–4)*

Sadly, society's utter lack of self-control to the point of devious immorality is on full display everywhere we look.

Lasciviousness

G766 *aselgeia*; licentiousness (sometimes including other vices):— filthy, wantonness

The multisyllabic word *lasciviousness* found in the long list of works of the flesh a Christian is to shun (Galatians 5:19) means *licentiousness*, another mouthful of a word. Licentious in *Merriam-Webster's* means "marked by the absence of legal and moral restraints; hostile or offensive to accepted standards of conduct; lewdness."

> *And lest, when I come again, my God will humble me among you, and that I shall bewail many which have sinned already, and have not repented of the uncleanness and fornication and lasciviousness which they have committed. (2 Corinthians 12:21)*

> *For when they speak great swelling words of vanity, they allure through the lusts of the flesh, through much wantonness, those that were clean escaped from them who live in error. (2 Peter 2:18)*

The word *wantonness* found in Romans 13:13 and 2 Peter 2:18 comes from the same Greek word *aselgeia* (G766) that *lasciviousness* comes from. Worldly people live wanton by living in pleasure or pursuing that which is sensual. "Ye have lived in pleasure on the earth, and been wanton; ye have nourished your hearts, as in a day of slaughter" (James 5:5). Paul told us these people are past feeling or past feeling any moral compunction, and have given themselves over to that which merely feels good to them at any given time. "Who being past feeling have given themselves over unto lasciviousness, to work all uncleanness with greediness" (Ephesians 4:19).

And Jude told us there would be "certain men crept in unawares . . . ungodly men, turning the grace of our God into lasciviousness, and denying the only Lord God, and our Lord Jesus Christ" (Jude 1:4). If they crept in, that means they were able to fool believers into letting them in, fooling them into accepting their Christian label. These men (and women) wanted to be accepted as Christians, but they denied Christ by how they lived, and they promoted all manner of evil in the name of tolerance.

Nigh

H7126 *qārab*; to *approach*, (bring near) for whatever purpose:— be at hand, make ready

H5066 *nāgaš*; to *be* or *come near* (for any purpose):— bring forth, give place, go near, overtake

H7138 *qārób*; *near* (in place, kinship, or time):— at hand, next, shortly

H7607 *šě ēr*; *flesh*, as living or for food; figuratively *kindred* by blood:— body, near of kin

H7131 *qārēb*; *near*:— come near, draw near

H7934 *šākēn*; a resident; fellow-*citizen*:— inhabitant, neighbor

H5060 *nāga*; to *touch*, i.e. *lay the hand upon*; by implication to *reach*; violently, to *strike*:— bring down, join, reach up

H369 *ayin*; to *be nothing* or *not exist*; a *non-entity*:— else, be gone, nor anything, unsearchable, well-nigh, without

G1448 *engizō*; to make *near*, i.e. *approach*:— be at hand, come (draw) near

G3844 *para*; properly *near*, i.e. *from beside, at* (or *in*) the *vicinity* of:— above, against, among, by, nigh unto

G1451 *engys*; *near*, (literally or figuratively, of place or time):— at hand, near, ready

G4314 *pros*; a preposition of direction; *forward* to, i.e. *toward, by the side of*, i.e. *near to*:—at, according to, among, between, by, whereby, unto

G4331 *prosengizō* from G4314 and G1448; to *approach near*:— come nigh

We could straight substitute the word *near* for *nigh* and be pretty safe in our interpretation of the verses that use this word, as in, "The Lord is nigh unto all them that call upon him, to all that call upon him in truth" (Psalm 145:18.) But there are a few subtle nuances to explore. The only verse that uses the H396 definition of *nigh* is Psalm 73:

"But as for me, my feet were almost gone; my steps had well nigh slipped" (Psalm 73:2). Asaph opined that his life had very nearly slipped into nothingness by his own doubts and sins and grievances due to the wicked in his midst. But a life that honors God has hope as he later penned: "Nevertheless I am continually with thee: thou hast holden me by my right hand. Thou shalt guide me with thy counsel, and afterward receive me to glory" (Psalm 72:23–24).

Vine's Complete Expository Dictionary assigns *Strong's* number G3897 to the phrase "nigh unto" (meaning *nearly resembling*) in Philippians 2:27, which is a clearer definition regarding Paul's retelling of Epaphroditus's sickness that almost cost him his life, whereas the King James Version translators chose G1448, meaning to *draw near*. Nearly resembling death makes much more sense.

And in Mark 5:11 we read: "Now there was there nigh unto the mountains a great herd of swine feeding." These swine were not simply "near" the mountain, but physically "on the side of" it (G4314).

Perdition + Pernicious

G684 *apōleia*; *ruin* or *loss* (physical, spiritual, or eternal):— damnation, destruction, perish, waste

Both words *perdition* (G684, noun) and *pernicious* (G684, adjective) come from the Greek word *apoleia*. Peter warned the brethren about destructive false teachers among us who, for their own glory, would sway many believers to that which was untrue about Christ and Christianity.

And many shall follow their pernicious ways; by reason of whom the way of truth shall be evil spoken of. (2 Peter 2:2)

The oxymoronic Christian feminist with her self-righteous reasonings or the female preacher with her seductive presentation claims to be Christian, but does not live out Christ's teachings. She ignores the truth in Scripture so she doesn't have to submit herself and her aspirations to Christ. We women must, through prayer, awareness, and diligent study of God's Word, keep ourselves from being fooled by those who live in perdition. "But we are not of them who draw back unto perdition; but of them that believe to the saving of the soul" (Hebrews 10:39).

Propitiation

G2435 *hilastērion*; an *expiatory* (place or thing), i.e. (concretely) an atoning *victim*, or (specifically) the *lid* of the Ark (in the Temple):— mercyseat
G2434 *hilasmos*; *atonement*, i.e. (concretely) an *expiator*:— propitiation

Jesus Christ is He:

Whom God hath set forth to be a propitiation through faith in his blood, to declare his righteousness for the remission of sins that are past, through the forbearance of God;
To declare, I say, at this time his righteousness: that he might be just, and the justifier of him which believeth in Jesus. (Romans 3:25–26)

There are three instances of the word *propitiation* found in the New Testament (See also 1 John 2:2 and 4:10). But for better understanding, we need to open the box within the box, to illuminate the definitions within the definition of this word. Expiatory means "one having the power to atone for," and atone means to "make amends for" some wrongdoing. In Romans 5:11 we read, "And not only so, but we also joy in God through our Lord Jesus Christ, by whom we have now received the atonement." Atonement

(G2643)—an undeserved yet beautiful "exchange" and "restoration to (the divine) favor"—is given to the repentant because of what our savior has done. Propitiation is only possible through Christ's blood (Hebrews 9:22) and is what reconciles us to God, the Father.

The last intriguing meaning of propitiation is *mercyseat* (G2435), which was the lid of the "ark of the covenant overlaid round about with gold" housed in the inner sanctuary of the tabernacle called the Holiest of all (Hebrews 9:3–4). The inner sanctuary and the ark of the covenant with its mercyseat mentioned once in Hebrews 9:5, were the physical "expiatory place and thing" to which the high priest once a year offered a blood sacrifice for all the people to God. But these physical things were the mere shadows of things to come and gave way to the Holiest of all—the righteous and merciful Son of God, and His atoning work for us. God gave us direct access to Himself through His ultimate mercyseat, Jesus Christ.

> *But Christ being come an high priest of good things to come, by a greater and more perfect tabernacle, not made with hands, that is to say, not of this building; Neither by the blood of goats and calves, but by his own blood he entered in once into the holy place, having obtained eternal redemption for us.*
> *(Hebrews 4:11–12)*

Purloining

G3557 *nosphizomai*; to *sequestrate* for oneself, i.e. *embezzle*:— keep back

Exhort servants to be obedient unto their own
masters, and to please them well in all things; not
answering again;
Not purloining, but shewing all good fidelity; that
they may adorn the doctrine of God our Saviour in
all things. (Titus 2:9–10)

If we take supplies from an employer without asking or "cook the books" by manipulating funds entrusted to us, we would be doing what the KJV describes as purloining. The same G3557 definition is used in Acts 5:2–3 to refer to what Ananias and his wife, Sapphira, did. Their "keeping back" was the *truth* about the full amount of their land sold, not the money itself. Had they told the truth and presented to the apostles what they wanted to give out of what was rightly theirs, there would have been no argument and no sudden graves dug.

Raca

G4469 *rhaka* of Aramaic origin; O *empty one*, i.e. thou *worthless* (as a term of utter vilification):— Raca

[W]hosoever is angry with his brother without a
cause shall be in danger of the judgment: and
whosoever shall say to his brother, Raca, shall be in
danger of the council: but whosoever shall say, Thou
fool, shall be in danger of hell fire. (Matthew 5:22)

Christ's warning in Matthew spotlights our relationships with our fellow brothers and sisters in Christ. How do we view and treat those that rub us the wrong way with their quirks or who don't believe secondary matters precisely as we do? They are Christ's beloved nonetheless even with their difficult personalities that may irritate us. They have as much to learn in their Christian journey of faith and obedience as we do. We might be tempted to defame or condemn them in our minds (or out loud!), but we please God when we extend patience and forgiveness and show them grace as Christ does for us.

Regeneration

G3824 *palingenesia*; (spiritual) *rebirth* (the state or the act), i.e. (figuratively) spiritual *renovation*; specially Messianic *restoration*:— regeneration

> *And Jesus said unto them, "Verily I say unto you, That ye which have followed me, in the regeneration when the Son of man shall sit in the throne of his glory, ye also shall sit upon twelve thrones, judging the twelve tribes of Israel." (Matthew 19:28)*

The regeneration Christ is speaking about is the "Messianic restoration," the fulfillment of God's plan for mankind that starts at the millennium when Christ overthrows all powers and governments and rules as King on earth with His saints beside Him.

In Titus 3:4–6, we read that God's kindness and love in saving us is not because of any righteous works we might claim, but by His mercy, the "washing of regeneration," and the "renewing of the Holy Ghost" within us.

The washing of regeneration refers to our baptism (G3067 washing: *bath, baptism*), to our being cleansed from past sins and to our spiritual renovation accomplished solely through God's Holy Spirit. As we emerge from the water, we are renewed! We become new creatures, and instead of the disarray our souls were in before, our spiritual houses are now in order. Praise God.

Sabaoth

G4519 *sabaōth* of Hebrew origin taken from H6635; *armies*, a military epithet of God:— sabaoth

> *And as Esaias said before, Except the Lord of Sabaoth had left us a seed, we had been as Sodoma, and been made like unto Gomorrha. (Romans 9:29)*

> *Behold, the hire of the labourers who have reaped down your fields, which is of you kept back by fraud, crieth: and the cries of them which have reaped are entered into the ears of the Lord of sabaoth. (James 5:4)*

The word *sabaoth* is found twice in the New Testament and is the transliteration (the converting of letters phonetically from one language to another) of the Hebrew word *saba* (H6635) meaning a mass of persons or an army. God is the God of armies or hosts composed of His mighty angels (Genesis 32:2). The Bible uses the phrase *Lord of hosts* or *Lord God of hosts* at least 278 times in the Old Testament. Angels not only worship God in glorious praise and obey His holy edicts, but they also minister to and protect us, God's children.

Safe

G804 *asphelēs*; *secure* (literally or figuratively):— certain, certainty, sure

There are five Hebrew definitions (H983, H7965, H3467, H7682, H6403) and two Greek definitions (G5195, G1295) found in *Strong's Concordance* that follow the expected meaning of the word *safe*: a refuge, having health, prosperity, and peace, to be open and free, to be lofty and inaccessible, and cause to escape, to preserve, to rescue.

But there is one use of safe (G804) found in Philippians chapter 3 that doesn't follow these definitions.

> *Finally, my brethren, rejoice in the Lord. To write the same things to you, to me indeed is not grievous, but for you it is safe. (Philippians 3:1)*

Paul made a point to the Philippian church that when we read repeated information about God, His goodness, and our natural response to Him, it never gets old. It is a sure thing, full of certainty. There is never a time or place in our earthly lives where we won't need encouragement or gentle prodding to keep going in faith and obedience. Paul used the same G804 word *asphelēs* in Hebrews 6:19, except the KJV translators chose the word *sure* instead. Either way, godly consolation never gets old.

That by two immutable things, in which it was
impossible for God to lie, we might have a strong
consolation, who have fled for refuge to lay hold
upon the hope set before us:
Which hope we have as an anchor of the soul, both
sure and stedfast, and which entereth into that within
the veil. (Hebrews 6:18–19)

Variance

G1369 *dichazō*; to *make apart*, i.e. *sunder* (figuratively
alienate):— set at variance
G2054 eris; a *quarrel*; i.e. (by implication) *wrangling*:—
contention, debate, strife

The word *variance* is found twice in the New Testament
both times with different meanings. In Matthew chapter 10,
Jesus Christ not only tells us He did not come here to bring
peace, He prepares us for the painful reality of being a
Christian in a non-Christian family.

For I am come to set a man at variance against his
father, and the daughter against her mother, and the
daughter in law against her mother in law.
And a man's foes shall be they of his own
household. (Matthew 10:35–36)

"Set at variance" (G1369) means to *alienate* or cause to
split apart. This is what happens to couples, whole families,
business partnerships, religious organizations, and nations
who do not believe the same things regarding morality,

religion, or politics. They cannot reconcile their vast chasm of differences in their man-made policies or man-made religious ideals.

This variance is especially taxing for an individual who loves their family but refuses to bend when it comes to God-made truths—especially the Truth Himself—and therefore finds themself in a broken one.

As mentioned earlier, Galatians 5:19–21 displays a long list of works of the flesh: "Adultery, fornication, uncleanness, lasciviousness, idolatry, witchcraft, hatred, variance, emulations, wrath, strife, seditions, heresies, envyings, murders, drunkenness and revellings." It is wise for us to know what these unfamiliar words mean so we avoid engaging in these behaviors and steer clear of those who do because "they which do such things shall not inherit the kingdom of God."

We learned what *emulations* and *lasciviousness* meant, but what about *variance*? Have you ever known a person who loved to stir the pot, so to speak, who deliberately caused trouble by making an issue out of nothing? People who aren't happy unless they're complaining about something or who find pleasure in being argumentative are people who excel at variance.

But we have our own list of words in Galatians 5:22 and 23, luscious fruit-of-the-Spirit words to live by and to excel at:

❀ Love
❀ Joy
❀ Peace

- ❀ Longsuffering [patience]
- ❀ Gentleness
- ❀ Goodness
- ❀ Faith
- ❀ Meekness [humility]
- ❀ Temperance [self-control]

These words embody who Christ is and are sweeter than honey and the honeycomb. When you live by them, you delight God because you are living by the Spirit of His Son.

May you, dear women, excel at these words and all the other God-fearing, God-honoring words in this study. By doing so, you declare God's Word is

More to be desired are they than gold, yea, than much fine gold: sweeter also than honey and the honeycomb. (Psalm 19:9–10)

Reader Quiz

It can be quite the challenge to keep all the definitions for these unusual KJV Bible words in the forefront of your memory. Below is a multiple-choice quiz to keep you sharp. Have fun! (Answer key on page 207.) How many did you guess correctly?

Note: As you have learned from reading this book, many word entries have several definitions depending on the context. For simplicity, I chose the most widely used definitions for each.

1. Admonish

O **a)** to be carried away, led away

O **b)** to draw near, approach

O **c)** to warn, caution

2. Beseech

O a) to request, to beg

O b) to build up, confirm

O c) to surround, protect, help

3. Bowels

○ a) cohabitation, bed

○ b) compassion, inward affection

○ c) peak, power, projection

4. Conversation

○ a) behavior, conduct

○ b) to know/not know, to see, be aware

○ c) to quarrel, debate, split apart

5. Edify

○ a) build up, confirm

○ b) secure, certain, sure

○ c) be needful, be bound

6.1 Ensue

○ a) to warn, to caution

○ b) longing, illicit desire

○ c) to pursue, persecute

6.2 Eschew

○ a) wrangle, contend, struggle

○ b) to shun, avoid

○ c) feign, hypocrisy

7. Exhort

○ a) array, put on, clothe with

○ b) embezzle, keep back

○ c) to entreat, to implore

8. Meet

○ a) secure, certain, sure

○ b) suitable, fitting, aid

○ c) longing, illicit desire

9. Nought

○ a) for nothing, in vain

○ b) wantonness, filthy

○ c) to shun, avoid

10. Perfect

○ a) to be clean, innocent, blameless, act manly

○ b) sound mind, self-controlled, discreet

○ c) complete, entire, whole

11. Quick-Quicken

O a) suitable, fitting, aid

O b) heat, zeal, ardor, excite

O c) alive, to live, to revive

12. Quit

O a) to be clean, innocent, blameless, act manly

O b) without self-control, excess

O c) ruin, destruction, waste

13. Recompense-Recompense

O a) compassion, inward affection

O b) be needful, be bound

O c) compensation, requital, make amends, repay, restore

14. Repent

○ a) rebirth, renovation

○ b) turn back, compunction, reversal, think differently

○ c) to entreat, to implore

15. Sober

○ a) ruin, destruction, waste

○ b) of sound mind, self-controlled, discreet

○ c) crooked, perverse

16. Strait

○ a) narrow, distress, to press

○ b) for nothing, in vain

○ c) be carried away, led away

17. Strive

○ a) wrangle, contend, struggle

○ b) to quarrel, debate, split apart

○ c) to request, to beg

18. Succour

○ a) behavior, conduct

○ b) rebirth, renovation

○ c) to surround, protect, help

19. Wist/Wit/Wot

○ a) to pursue, persecute

○ b) to know/not know, to see, be aware

○ c) worthless, empty one

20. Behoved

O a) suitable, fitting, aid

O b) be necessary, be bound

O c) to be clean, innocent, blameless, act manly

21. Chambering

O a) cohabitation, bed

O b) array, put on, clothe with

O c) wrangle, contend, struggle

22. Concupiscence

O a) compassion, inward affection

O b) behavior, conduct

O c) longing, illicit desire

23. Condescend

O a) turn back, compunction, reversal, think differently

O b) be carried away, led away

O c) to warn, to caution

24. Convenient

O a) be necessary, be bound

O b) due season, fit, becoming

O c) complete, entire, whole

25. Dissimulation

O a) feign, hypocrisy

O b) ruin, destruction, waste

O c) alive, to live, to revive

26. Emulation

O a) to request, to beg

O b) complete, entire, whole

O c) heat, zeal, ardor, excite

27. Endued

O a) array, put on, clothe with

O b) compensation, requital, make amends, repay, restore

O c) atonement, make amends

28. Froward

O a) crooked, perverse

O b) worthless, empty one

O c) alive, to live, to revive

29. Horn

○ a) armies, mass of persons

○ b) peak, power, projection

○ c) narrow, distress, to press

30. Incontinent/Incontinency

○ a) heat, zeal, ardor, excite

○ b) without self-control, excess

○ c) crooked, perverse

31. Lasciviousness

○ a) to entreat, to implore

○ b) for nothing, in vain

○ c) wantonness, filthy

32. Nigh

○ a) narrow, distress, to press

○ b) near, draw near, approach

○ c) to surround, protect, help

33. Perdition + Pernicious

○ a) ruin, destruction, waste

○ b) feign, hypocrisy

○ c) be carried away, led away

34. Propitiation

○ a) due season, fit, becoming

○ b) near, draw near, approach

○ c) atonement, make amends

35. Purloining

○ a) without self-control, excess

○ b) cohabitation, bed

○ c) embezzle, keep back

36. Raca

○ a) worthless, empty one

○ b) for nothing, in vain

○ c) heat, zeal, ardor, excite

37. Regeneration

○ a) build up, confirm

○ b) rebirth, renovation

○ c) atonement, make amends

38. Sabaoth

O a) peak, power, projection

O b) armies, mass of persons

O c) complete, entire, whole

39. Safe

O a) secure, certain, sure

O b) due season, fit, becoming (convenient)

O c) build up, confirm

40. Variance

O a) wantonness, filthy

O b) to quarrel, debate, split apart

O c) to pursue, persecute

Answer Key

1. c	21. a
2. a	22. c
3. b	23. b
4. a	24. b
5. a	25. a
6.1 c	26. c
6.2 b	27. a
7. c	28. a
8. b	29. b
9. a	30. b
10. c	31. c
11. c	32. b
12. a	33. a
13. c	34. c
14. b	35. c
15. b	36. a
16. a	37. b
17. a	38. b
18. c	39. a
19. b	40. b
20. b	

About the Author

Gleniece Lytle is a writer, editor, and Bible study enthusiast. Being a curious Christian woman, she puzzled over the unusual words she found while reading her KJV Bible and after much research, eventually wrote a popular series for her blog, Desert Rain. Gleniece also writes a monthly newsletter, *Abide & Blossom*, to uplift the weary Christian woman living in the chaos of our times. When not writing, she serves nonfiction authors with her editing and typesetting business, Desert Rain Editing.

Gleniece lives in Arizona in an unfinished desert cabin with Douglas, her husband of over forty years. She homeschooled all five of her children and loved learning something new every day along with them. Contemplating the goodness of God, like gazing at the rich palette of a desert sunset, always leaves her awe-struck. Faith and obedience to Christ has turned her once parched life into a well-watered garden. She's happiest with a glass of red wine, a piece of dark chocolate, and is positively giddy when a graceful pirouette of words perfectly captures what she struggled with for days leaps onto the page and bows.

You can connect with Gleniece at desertraingleniece.com, sign up for her monthly newsletter, *Abide & Blossom*, and visit desertrainediting.com for your nonfiction editing and typesetting needs.